I couldn't breathe. I woke up gasping for precio
flung my legs over the side of the bed and sat up. I finally, I was able to suck in
sweet oxygen. If, lying down makes you breathless and you aren't even running in
your dreams, it quickly gets your attention.
Sarah rolled over and asked if I was alright.
  "Yes, honey, I'm fine, get some sleep. Your car's picking you up in three hours"
She said,
  "I'm scared."
  "About making your flight?
  "No, about you."
I was probably lying when I said,
  "Don't worry; I'll be fine."
By the time the car picked Sarah up, I had passed out sitting in a chair that, believe
me, was anything but a Barcalounger. The only way I could sleep was sitting up.
After Sarah left for her flight, I looked up my symptoms online only to discover that I
was in the throes of Congestive Heart Failure.
At 8:03 a.m. I put the Lime in the Coconut, called the Doctor, woke him up and said,
  "Doctor!!! Is there something I can take?"
My soft-spoken East Indian cardiologist said,
  "Yes, there is something you can take. You can take a drive to my office as soon
as
  it is probable for you to do so."
Sarah, was winging her way to choreograph one of her Royal Caribbean Ice Skating
Shows in St. Thomas. We had discussed whether or not she should take this gig
leaving me on my own, but I insisted that she take it. Sarah in turn, asked my sister
Linda, to fly out from New Jersey, as she had sensed I was a bit wonky and
unquestionably not my usually buoyant, deliriously effervescent, self. So, Linda and
I drove to Dr. D's offices, where the first order of business was an Ultra Sound.
There was the predictable prodding and poking and, of course, that always
unnecessarily cold blue jelly. Instead of watching the fuzzy black and white video
screen. I always watch the Lab Tech, Rusty's face. When he grimaced, and his
eyes widened in shock, I knew the news would not be good. Indeed, Rusty, a gay
Hells Angel Biker Bear, who could get fired for saying so, told me that my heart
muscle's Ejection Fraction was down to 10% or less. For the last 12 years, despite
the ravages of my ever-lovin' Myocardial Infarction, ominously called The Widow
Maker, I had defied the odds by sporting a 20% E.F. It's important to note that 50-
80% is typical. Whenever I arrived for an appointment with Dr. Babu, he would tell
me, in his melodious East Indian lilt,
  "It goes without staying that you are my miracle man. My other patients with your
  numbers barely get out of bed in the morning! You, my friend, speed through life
  like some kind of motor rooster!"
As the vision of my future as a motor rooster seared through my predictive logic, I
knew that I was either going to get a new heart or die with my, not so trusty, ol' fuel
pump. My god, what was I in for? I have no idea really, I just know that I want to
stick

1

around as long as I can. What the hell, whether I'm going to live or die, I don't want to miss a milli-second of this ride.

THURSDAY - 7/27/17

How did I manage to lose 75% of my heart function? Turns out the culprit was that ornery Myocardial Infarction, ominously dubbed, *The Widow Maker*, notorious for dropping one dead on the spot. I was on a passenger jet, cruising from Seattle to L.A. at 30,000 feet. It was August 10th, 2005, a Thursday, and I was the lucky one out of four, to have symptoms. This merry little medical miracle was evidenced the next day when at least 20 doctors stopped by to chat. I asked one of them,

"Why all the attention? I must have talked to every doctor in the joint this morning." In his best bedside manner, he explained,

"Well, Mr. Alcroft, you had a Widow Maker, and...simply put, we just don't get to talk

to many of you guys the day after, or ever for that matter."

I was starting to become enveloped by a warm abiding awareness of totally enjoying my current mortality; which at that very moment seemed obviously predicated upon on how quickly I might soon depart this magical planet Earth. I really like it here and I really want to stick around.

In the weeks that followed I felt not so great. I was weak, and I had developed a deep cough. Dr. Babu explained that my symptoms were the beginnings of CHF, Congestive Heart Failure. He sent me to Dr. James "Crazy Jimmy" Ong, for a look see. Despite his complete and total lack of a personality that at times would peak approaching vapidity, Dr. Ong is the top Pacemaker Physician in the area and he told me that his evaluation placed me in Stage 3 of Heart Failure. Whew, merely a Stage 3 status. I had some time to think about this impending implant. My ego jumped up and told me that I was too young to become the Bionic Man, so I arrogantly asked,

"Yeah, well thanks doctor, what is Stage 4?"
He casually offered,

"Oh, stage 4, is merely a euphemism for death,".

At my insistence, he installed a pacemaker in my chest the next day. Four -years later, my battery was getting low, so I got my second pacemaker. This time the technology

was four years better so, I decided I would spend the extra bucks and spring for XM/Sirius Radio and Climate Control. I also opted-in for OnStar, because I don't know where I am half the time and lately, I keep locking myself out of my bathrobe! On this particular Thursday, 12 years later, I find myself being told that ever with Ong's bionic booster, my heart function has fallen to a whopping 7%. Vishva offered,

"Call my associate Dr. Moriguchi. He is the Head of the Cardio Transplant unit at Cedars-Sinai, I've known him since we were at Georgetown together. You'll like him;

he is a true gentleman and a scallop, here's his number."
Hoping that he was going to correct himself I repeated,

"A true gentleman AND a scallop?"
"Indeed", affirmed my terminally malapropped cardiologist, "for all intentional purposes, he certainly is!"

I've got to meet this guy! I high tailed it out of Babu's office and before I got to the elevator I had Moriguchi's assistant, Steve, on the line. I told him of my plight and could hear him flipping through pages It seemed very retro.

"Let's see what we have Mr. Alcroft", Steve stalled,

"Okay, I found something. We have an opening in about three weeks. Will that work
for you?"

"Sure, great, will the morgue pick me up or should I just have my ashes Fed-Ex'd?"

"How's that?"

"I'm so sorry Steve, you'll have to excuse me. I'll get back with you, thanks for your help. I really appreciate you…"

I was suddenly in a dreamlike trance. My brain felt dull, unable to support thought. I called Vishva and in a defeated tone said,

"Dr. Babu, Steve I called Maraguchi and they can't see me for three weeks.
what the fuck am I going to do?"

Once again, he lilted,

"What you are going to the fuck do my friend is get yourself to Cedars Sinai Emergency and let them take it from there. It goes without staying, I will alert my associate Dr. Moriguchi that you are on the way. I told my sister what he'd said and when we returned home, Linda starting packing an overnight bag for me. I hopped into the shower. Linda was appalled as she yelled through the bathroom door,

"What the hell are you doing? He said RIGHT NOW!"

Savoring and finishing up my shower, which I surmised might have been my last, we got into the car. I insisted on driving; also, perhaps my last time behind the wheel.

Arriving at Cedars, I said to the receptionist,

"Hi, my doctor sent me over. Apparently, my heart is failing."

From behind the double layer of security glass and through that metal sink drain, she
muffled,

"What is your doctor's name sir?"

"Doctor Vishva Babu."

"What Hospital is he with?"

"He's the head of Cardiology at Los Robles. He recommended that I see Dr. Moriguchi."

She fiddled and fumbled through a pile of papers for thirty long seconds or so and then looked up at me as if she 'd never seen me before saying,

"How can I help you, sir?"

"Well, I believe my heart is probably still failing."

With no apparent reaction or eye contact she offered me a clip board.

"Have a seat and fill this out. What was your doctor's name?"

"What, was it? Do you mean before OR after he entered the physician relocation program?"

Blank stare. Humor was apparently not part of her job description. To be fair, when people who should be paying attention to me because it's their job, aren't paying attention to me when I am dying, I become a bit of an asshole. I breathed in through my nose and out through my mouth three times, it always works. With feigned cheer I brightly stated.

"His name is Dr. Moriguchi, and he's head of the Cardio Transplant Unit."

4

"Please have a seat. I'll see if I can locate him."

I filled out and signed all of the papers in about the same amount of time it had taken me to complete my SATs in 1967. I must say that as soon as I turn in my paperwork, they pretty much immediately got me on a gurney. I knew that my journey, my gurney journey, was just beginning, or not. My head always throws those last two words at me, every time I think about all of this journey stuff. I'm going to find distractions; lots of distractions. I hope I'm going to be here as long as it takes me to get a new ticker. I 'm going to try to make sure I make real contact with everyone I meet. This person hovering over me and then the next person touching me with a hand or a needle, might be the last face I ever see. In an effort to shrug off the looming veil of kickin' it, I'm taking full advantage of the name tags. They present a welcomed challenge for my visually cognitive powers. Case in point; if a nurse's hair is covering her tag, how can I work to my audient if I don't know her name? I told her that her hair would look terrific pulled back. They always pull their hair back to show me what it would look like, appeasing the dying old man who now knows their name! A-ha! I knew where I was going, I just didn't know how long this was going to take and was this going to be my reality? As I glided on my gurney, I couldn't help but think of all those hospital shows where the quickly moving foam-tiled ceilings are rapidly punctuated by fluorescent lights passing swiftly over one's face. That is my face they were flashing above today, Jesus! I am, by god, going to be on a first name basis with everyone! They're tough crowds, they've heard it all! I'll try to never let anyone of my species leave the room without a laugh. Somehow, I was calmly accepting my fate. I was banished to the Hallway Inn, as my ever-clever son, Thatcher, has dubbed it. I laid there, obediently, for what seemed to be an eternity. It became four, then six hours. Again, I'm going to have to wait for someone to die! I started imagining myself getting a shopping cart and setting up a plastic tarp around my space. I finally got a room in the Cardio Transplant ICU, which I soon learned is the Motel 6 of Cedars. *"Come on Down, we'll leave the seat up for you."* I meet Maraguchi three weeks later when he was making his morning rounds. He had no idea who I was but he did think he might have maybe remembered a guy named Vishva.

I laughed a lot today. It's not that I've been telling myself jokes I've never heard before or even jokes that I had heard before but just never told quite that way. I've actually, been thinking about my wife and children and all of the joy they have given me. They are my life force and all of the reasons I want this much needed new heart. Oh, I know, full well that, someone has to die so that I might live. I've tried to rationalize this, as I struggle to make sense of it all. My ragged hypothesis is that anyone's death will be an event quite separate from me; out of my hands and beyond my control. My

death will not be a given or an accident because I have actively sought to embrace this hope and admittedly my last desperate touchstone of control as I stay here and wait, patiently, like the perfect patient should. I wish I could remember all of my memories. A new heart won't help that. It's curious how we attribute love and emotion to our ticker. Of course, thoughts and memories don't reside in the heart. When people feel emotion, they put their hands on their chests, indicating the spirit, they are feeling from their core. Although it is all around us, the energy feels focused on our ever-beating essence of love, joy and inner peace, the heart chakra. I guess I could cry tonight but I can't because I'm smiling too hard, thinking about Thatcher. When he was very young, and just discovering language, he would say something hilariously insightful, sarcastic or just plain goofy. Sarah and I would look at each other thinking

it might have just been a fluke. We know better now. The funny came naturally to Thatch, as does sleep for me right now

SATURDAY – 7/29/17

What a day! More prodding and poking. To wit, they've concluded that I indeed need a new heart and will be submitted as a candidate to be put on the list for a new heart

and now, surprise, a new liver; a double whammy, that might as well be a trifecta because it turns out Cedars has a strict double transplant cutoff age of 65. I am 68.

Upon hearing this tidbit, before my morning tea, was another little stomach dropper on this most ginormous emotional roller coaster of my life. I immediately started to imagine my options which seemed to be dwindling as rapidly as my luck. What is luck

anyway? Is it some sort of God given ability, an innate gyroscope that enables one with the power to have good things happen all the time? Being sent home to die doesn't seem like I'm on a particularly lucky streak, but I am. I'm lucky enough to have

lived my life just about exactly the way I've always wanted to. Luckier still after having

some wonderfully romantic and loving relationships to have my breath taken away by

a beautiful Japanese ice skater. How lucky can I guy be? I'll tell you how lucky. She is by my side as I write. She is a wonder woman and I wonder what she sees in me?

I've also been thinking how lucky I am to be experiencing something like a flipping' Heart Transplant! How many people can say that someone else's heart is beating in their chest? How many can say they have received the gift of life, twice!

Well, the way things are going. Apparently not me. I was feeling pretty damn sorry for myself until around dinner-time, when my nightly assortment of inedibles arrived. I thought of the great spaghetti and fish and Oh My God salads that I grew up on at Ange's Boulevard Tavern in Youngstown Ohio, I thought of my sister, Cindy who still lives close to Youngstown, and the Boulevard and how she lives close to Cleveland. I wonder what the Cleveland Clinic would say? I jumped on the internet, and found that both The Mayo and Cleveland Clinics have cut-offs for dual transplants at 70. I'm hatching a plan. The next time my Transplant Team shows up I'm going to request that my records be sent to both of those clinics, making my team aware that I'm aware I have some options. Cedars isn't the only game in town although they are in town and they are the best in the world, of all hospitals anywhere at organ transplants. Essentially, I'm bluffing. My liver specialist, Dr. Shaye, came in today and told me that my liver is functioning perfectly but still needs to be replaced due to the scarring, likely from the 12 years of abuse it has endured from my 20% heart, with no idea how long I've been at 7%. It's called Heart Induced Cirrhosis and, yes, it shows up as the dreaded "C" word on my record. I asked if the cirrhosis had been caused by my years of free-drinks in the Comedy Clubs, and he said,

"No, your heart is more than likely the culprit."

"You mean I could have drunk more? Why wasn't I told?"

He chuckled but still insisted they will, by God, get me a new heart and a new liver, hold the onions. Great news, just as I was starting to think my chances of seeing my next birthday was going to be severely impacted. Five minutes later my cardio guy, Dr. Evan Kransdorf, eyes glued to the floor, told me that my case would be presented on August 4th to a Board of 30 Doctors, surgeons, social workers, psychiatrists and wealthy donors; not necessarily the organ type mind you. He lamented that my chances didn't look terrific. They had never made an exception. Was this going to be *The Inquisition, The Nuremberg Trials*, or just a good old fashion lynching? It didn't look good for me because of my age and now the C word, my scarred and scarlet letter. My Team would deliver the verdict to me on the morning of the 4th. It wasn't going to be easy for me or for them to get or give this potentially broken news but I am ready. I mean, what choice do I have? C'est la vie ou la mort, simplement comme ca?

SUNDAY – 7/30/17

So, now I'm living moment by moment, with an uncertain judgment looming. The outcome is going to be a surprise no matter which way it goes. This morning Sarah pointed out that my eight I.V. bags had magically diminished to a mere five overnight.

A nurse came in this afternoon and silently disconnected two more. I'm down to three

I.V. bags. They are prepping me for early discharge in five days' time when my

evaluation descends from above, from below. I lay back on my pillow and my thoughts drifted to the day before my irritating little *Widow Maker* in 2005. We had just spent our yearly visit with my wife's parents, Hede and her stepmother, Nellie, in verdant and temperate Kelowna, British Columbia. There is a Japanese population there that moved back from Toronto and various camps after the war, exacting their revenge by buying up all of the cherry, apple and peach orchards. The Canadian Government erred on the side of goofiness when they relocated their Japanese population of British Columbia, inland. After all, Kelowna is 270 miles from the coast and the Nipponese patriots could have signaled those Japanese subs and warships far too easily from that distance! Then, after the Second World War was brought to an abrupt end by the First Nuclear War, Canada allowed them to move back to Kelowna where they could, at least, wave to their relatives. "Konnichiwa". They quickly snatched up most of the apple, peach and cherry orchards in British Columbia and an amazingly vibrant Japanese Community emerged. The climate, soil and exceptional growing season created a cultural cavalcade of ever visiting friends or relatives, bringing along homegrown produce. Coronation Grapes, Tomatoes, Radishes, Carrots, and Apples of all varieties would be exchanged and prepared in a calming sense of serenity. Hede, my father in law, had an apple tree in his backyard on which he had grafted and was growing five varietal pommes. When Sarah's mother passed away, they were living in Toronto. Her father took an ad out in the classified section, "Japanese widower and his 12-year-old daughter seek a housekeeper who cooks Japanese style. Contact Hede Kawahara." Several days later Hede received a phone call and the Japanese accented voice on the other end said, "I'm recently divorced and interested in the position. Do you, by any chance, know the Hede Kawahara that graduated from Kelowna High School before the war?" Well, of course, he did because he was, he or this anecdote wouldn't be worth the parchment it's scribed upon. He gave her the job, and three years later he and Nellie were married. Sarah and Nellie got along then and love each other very much now. Hede passed in 2014 but we still visit Nellie each year. Food rules in Kelowna; my wife's relatives always prepare special "Jamie" variations of their native Culinary Fare and I genuinely do appreciate it as the food is delicious even sans animals. Their intentions are so sweet and pure and they are all so loving and attentive to Sarah's "White, Vegetarian" husband. One night I was savoring Yosh's Coronation Grape Pie and I asked her how in the world she made such delicious pie. She proudly announced it was her secret ingredient,

"Lard"!

I was in mid-bite but continued to deliver the fork out of love and courtesy I finished the pie knowing that the "lard" would surely work its way out of my body in a scant few decades. Yosh is a sweetie and her intentions are so innocently loving, even though she could have probably brought Bat Masterson to his knees at a game of Texas Hold 'em. As she has done to me many times!

I remember when I broke the news to our kids that we would be moving to Amsterdam. I tried to break it to them gently,

"Kids, times are tough, money's tight, so pick a straw, because we're going to have to let one of you go…"

Blank stare.

"Okay, kidding. Your mother is going to choreograph *Holiday on Ice* and we're going to get to live in Amsterdam for four months! Isn't that exciting?"

Collective groans, which, I guess, is better than a blank stare. I've known for years that Europeans hadn't invented inconvenience, they had merely perfected it. This was a fact my children were soon to discover. When we walked into our Amsterdam apartment it was a Cluster Feng Shui replete with clumps of hair in the furniture cushions and a partially gnawed T-bone under the couch. I silently hoped that the previous tenants had a dog. When we questioned the landlady, about the grunge, she proudly presented us the keys, accompanied by a cursory curtsy and explanation,

"This is Amsterdam, and we are Dutch."

Thank you I thought, now I won't have to bother whipping out my Rand-McNally!

"You may clean it up yourself or wait until Tuesday of course."

"But it's Wednesday, why will we have to wait until Tuesday?"

"Oh, Tuesday, of course, is Cleaning Day in Holland."

"Of course."

Thanks again.

The next day was a typical Amsterdam August day; 32 degrees C. (90 Fahrenheit) and such drenching humidity, I was tempted to jump into one of the canal's just to dry off! Thatcher and I were walking to the local Hardware store one day, and he said,

"Dad, it's so hot here, I can't stand it."

"Well, you know what they say, Thatcher?"

"Let's go back to California?"

"No, Sues Non calor sed umor est scriptor."

"Huh?"

"it's not the heat. It's the humidity."

"Why did we have to come here for some stupid Humidity? It's not much fun!"

"Sorry buddy'"

The first night Thatcher had been skeeter bit at least 10 million times (4 million centigrade). The heat dictated we leave the windows open, and they had no screens.

Easy fix, we found a hardware store where I was flatly told that they didn't have screens because Holland has no bugs. It was 90 degrees with stagnant, swan-guano

laden, canals meandering everywhere. Okay, no screens, a bit inconvenient but I can

adapt. I went to the fan aisle and mercifully saw the perfect fan. Well not quite perfect,

as it was the floor model. It had been running for god knows how long but I was undaunted! It was the perfect size for our screen-less window and well-priced. We unplugged it and carried it to the checkout counter. Handing it to the clerk, he looked at the fan, then to me,

"I'm sorry sir, we cannot sell dis fan, it is our flour mudel"

"I know, I unplugged it, and I love it, it's perfect."

"Vell, you are going to have to take it back and plog it bach sir."

"But, this is the fan I need, it's perfect!"

"Sourry, it's unly for display."

I paused for as long as I could, waiting for him to speak; nothing.

"When will you have more in stock?"

"Oh.... Probably not until May or Joon."

"It's September, why in the world do you need the flour muddle now?"

"That's our only flour muddle sir."

"Of course."

"Vee keep for selling display example, sir."

"For selling what Fer Cris-Sake?"

"Please watch your languages, sir!"

The store was empty.

"Okay, sorry. So, it's on display, to sell what may I ask? "

"Of course, you may....."

"What? May what?"

"Ask."

" Okay, for selling what?"

"For selling more fans, of course."

"Of course. More fans, more fans, of course! But not until next May, right?"

"Hopefolly, yes, next May, of course."

"Look, I'll pay you full price for this fan right now, even though it's probably been running," indicating Thatcher, "...for most of my son's childhood."

"Ah, yes, childhood, a beautiful time. You are Americans, of course?"

"Why do you say that, because I'm making a reasonable argument?"

"I'm afraad I'm not understanding dis, sir."

I grumped in earnest.

"How convenient."

"We make for our customer's convenience, no?"

"Of course. No. No, of course. Vell Danke"

"Graag gedaan and thank you, sir, come again."

"Of course, I will. See you in May!"

We started off for home without screens or a fan, but before we did, I took Thatcher to get an ointment to relieve his itching at the Apoteek where I was summarily scolded

that they had no unguent to relieve itching because they, of course, have no bugs in Holland. I could, of course, buy cortisone. Cortisone! What no Percocet? Or Heroin? Apparently, that may have been an option because I saw that they did have syringes.

Alas, they were probably the flour muddels and I'd already lost that battle! Walking away with my Dalmatian-Boy, I mumbled something about, the god-damned Dutch and their lousy god-damned attitudes. We took a few steps and through the din of itching Thatcher asked,

"Hey Dad, marijuana is legal here in Holland, right?"

12

Trying not to stumble over my flabbergastation, I casually answered,
  "Why yes Thatcher, it is."
In a few more steps he said,
  "And prostitution too, right?"
  Uh…sure..
We both looked straight ahead as we walked. He casually looked up, offering,
  "Man, what do you got to do to make these people happy?"

I passed out writing last night, woke up early this morning, went back to sleep and started having nightmares. There were giant mosquitos and itchy boys in lederhosen, with donkey ears and they were smoking cigars. What I had last night didn't necessarily feel like sleep at all. They are going to have to put me on a Sominex drip, adding to the I.V. bags that are daily disappearing from my I.V. Tree. What am I really going to be going through here? This is getting serious. Will someone else's heart

beat in my ribcage, consorting with the very same liver, it grew up with? There's another medical tidbit! I've been told that the organs have to come from the same donor and that I could be one out of 220 dual transplant recipients in the U.S. I serial napped today, thinking about all of that sad and scary stuff between my REM's, struggling to keep those nagging thoughts of mortality, that spell trouble, under control. Hell, I do 5 or 6 "shows" a day in here, turning it on for all of the doctors, surgeons, shrinks, social workers that do their 'Knock & Walk' into my room. I figure if these are my last days I want to have and leave a lot of smiles and laughter. To partially quote Mavis Levrer, "…to skid in sideways, totally worn out, shouting, Holy Shit, what a ride!"

If something goes down that I'm able to control, I throw myself into pursuing whatever

I must, to resolve what I'm facing and hope for the best outcome. Oh, I might worry, feel anxiety or pace the floor but I will do my due diligence to find a solution; evidenced

by getting myself to Dr. Babu when I was feeling so poorly. However, if it's something

like waiting for someone's heart to walk through the door, so to speak, that is entirely

out of my hands. I surrender to the fates and whatever else may enter into that plethora of unknown variables. Hard and fast constants lingering in the fluctuating values of my current collective, existential equation. I've been told that some people wait for a new heart for as long as 16 months, sometimes three years. One previous recipient, who's had his new pump for six years, Mason Summers, told me that he had total organ failure before his heart finally arrived. We as a nation are so bad about donating. My situation is exacerbated by the fact that my blood type is O+. That makes me a universal donor but not a getter because O+ is a trendy model and applicable to all blood types. I'm considering moving to a state with no Helmet Laws.   We moved a lot when I was a kid. I've only moved my family once and when we did I remember we had a pile of Good Will Donations in the corner of the garage and my middle daughter, 5-year-old Hayley, who is now a touring pop star, film/television actress and dynamic businesswoman asked me what that pile of stuff was. I explained,

   "We're going to give it away to less fortunate people by donating it to Good Will."
Her eyebrows furrowed,
   "Give it away? For Free!?
   "Of course, honey, it's a Donation. We're giving it away."
She flatly insisted,
   "Not if I can sell it first."

On Saturday afternoon she set up a yard sale, and I noticed that a beloved beaded Indian belt buckle and her well cuddled stuffed Barney were among the offerings. She
loved Barney so much that at dinner every night we had to sing, "I love you, You love
me…etc."
I queried,
  "Hayley, that's your Barney and your beaded Navajo belt buckle. You don't want to
  sell those do you?"
  "Not really," she patiently explained, "but, you know Daddy if you don't put out some
  good stuff, they won't buy the junk."
On Saturday she recruited two of her most shapely 7-year-old friends to don their bikini's and go to the corner waving two signs, "GOING OUT OF BIZNESS, EVERY THING MUST GO!" and "LICKWADATING SALE, TODAY ONLY!". She, of course, had worked out an agreeable percentage deal with her bathing beauties. She was five and already channeling Dale Carnegie. Before I nod off, I must report that today I was blessed with a Swan-Ganz which they implanted directly and not so delicately, into my neck. It follows an arterial path into the right side of my heart which has increased to 3 times its normal size to compensate for the left side which is, as Dr. Babu would put it, 'for all intentional purposes, dead.' If the occasion should arise that they have to get drugs to my heart lickety-split, it's my own little Heart Pool Lane. It turns out that for fear of infection I can't leave my room until they find me a heart. Tonight's episode is called, The Tale of the Tell-Tale Catheter. I suspect my I.V. Tree, which I have vowed to one-day wheel around the world promoting donor ship, has been implanted with a tracking device, so I am indeed trapped. I just looked outside, and there is a white van, with a dish on the roof, parked below my window. I knew that they would find me someday. Do me a favor; go tap on the window and tell them to go get some coffee. I'm in for the night.

There are creatures, posing as humans, who randomly stalk the hospital halls. They are easy to spot as they wear light blue Cuban shirts. I'm told they call themselves 'Volunteers'. Typically, they are actual humans who are grateful for the new life they, or their significant others have been given, and they want to give back in some way or another. One wonderful volunteer is Susie, a jolly little lady, much in the mold of one of the fairy godmothers in Disney's animated Cinderella. She and her former, but still best friend, husband traveled the world collecting and selling old books, including ancient leather-bound incunabula's. Susie crotchets little red hearts and passes them out to those who are waiting for a heart. We have struck up a friendship; a relatively easy thing to do with your fairy godmother. She visits every Saturday and is never at a loss for words and great stories. We both share a love of photography, primarily our own, and we swap photos and tales of exotic locales to pass the time. Last Saturday she related that in her eight years of volunteering, she has never visited anyone in the South Tower, where they house those waiting for a heart, that she hasn't then been able to visit, with their new organs, in the North Tower, the Happy Place. Sarah and I both credit her crocheted hearts with our buoyed spirits. She has infused my old heart with the strength to hang on and has given my, soon to be new heart hope of imminence. Other volunteers who are actual heart transplant recipients also stop by. Their mission is to listen to your story and answer any questions you might have about what you're going to experience pre- and post-op. One such overly eager commiserater is a fellow named Bill. On duty every Wednesday, Bill stopped to ask if I had any questions. I looked over at Sarah and before we could formulate a query he eagerly volunteered,
 "So, you a Dodger fan? I think they're going to go all the way this year. What I
   admire about those Dodgers is that none of them take a knee during the national
   anthem, no sir, not like those NFL turncoats."
Driven to divert this awkward and potentially combustible conversation I said,
 "Well Bill, I don't know what their right to freedom of expression has to do with me
   getting a heart and liver but..."
 "Oh my God!", he imploded,
 "A heart AND a liver? Oh boy, that's tough. I thought I had it tough but geez, I felt like I got hit by a truck but you, my friend, are going to feel like you got hit by a train!"
I mentally unfriended him,
 "Really Bill? I'm so glad you stopped by to make me feel so-o-o-o much better
   about this transplant thing. Now, I guess, I'll have nothing to fear other than
   unbearable, excruciating and unimaginable pain."
I wasn't in the mood for this guy.
 "Well James, don't take it the wrong way."
I wished I could get up and give "Wrong Way Bill" a well-placed knee. I broke my vow, as this member of my species did not leave with a laugh.

THURSDAY – 8/3/17

I guess I was a little rough on Volunteer Bill yesterday as I gallivanted through one of my prednisone induced tirades. Trust me; steroids are not our friends. Maybe Bill got *Debbie Downer's* heart but I am glad I'm in here for a gift from the Cardiac Gods. Glad it's nothing to do with my upper or lower tracts because the food, okay call it that if you must, has been abysmal, nay, inedible. The sole I had the other night was so leathery and overcooked that I chose to carve Desiderata into the skin for inspiration. I hung it on the wall behind my bed. Then I sent the veggies back because I suspected there might be a trace of nutrients left in them. A few nights ago, when they brought me a side of mashed potatoes with my Lasagna and bread, I guessed that they had decided it was time to "load me up" on carbs. I suspected that they'd signed me up for a marathon? Little do they know that I used to run in the NYC Marathon every November, but the crowds got too big and everyone seems to be in such a hurry. New York City is a beautiful city and, did you know, the route goes right through Central Park? I always take my camera and allow myself to soak in the sights and feed the Black Squirrels. People rush through the marathon experience. But for me, I stop for lunch at The Tavern, have a couple of drinks, and grab a room at The Carlyle, savoring the opulence. I like to try and figure out what to do with all of those pillows. BTW, I can't believe the deals to be had in that Mini-Bar. Where else can you get a Coke and a bag of chips for $37.50? When you run marathons my way, you'll find that by the second day, the crowds have really thinned out. I just heard on the 10 o'clock News that a man in Santa Rosa rushed into his burning house to rescue his Dad from the domestic inferno. Oh, wait a minute, I think I misheard. It wasn't his Dad; it was his Dad's ashes! What would the word for that be, redundant? I only say redundant because I've never been quite certain as to the correct use of irony, as opposed to something that is ironic. Redundant will have to do for tonight. More anon.

First thing this morning, Dr. Xie presented my case to the Cedars-Sinai Board of 30 doctors, surgeons, social workers, and psychiatrists. She pleaded that my numerical age was misleading and that I had been behaving very childishly. It did the trick because, wouldn't you know, they made an exception and granted me my double whammy. Sarah and I looked across the room from each other with tears welling in our eyes. I've always welcomed exceptions and acceptance. Exceptive acceptance, I love it! I was told that I would be best, and perhaps first served by staying at Cedars until a heart can be located. We had no idea how long it would be but at least now at least can re-decorate! I'll accept visitors but only if they've filled out their donor cards and they drive crazy fast to get here! I'm thinking of holding out for the heart of a 25-year-old pole-dancer who looks like a ho' but I may have to settle for the ticker of a 53–year-old Polish guy who operates a back-hoe. Who would have thunk I'd actually, be looking forward to being split open like a Christmas Goose? What!? Being what!? Bring my driver around!

This afternoon I had a liver biopsy, and the doctor gently leaned over me and said,

in a concerned tone,

"Mr. Alcroft, I'm your surgeon, Dr. Freeman. Before we begin the procedure, I must warn you that there is a chance of internal bleeding or even a stroke."

I looked at him concerned,

"For you or me?" His mask fluttered, I think with laughter; hard to tell.

When surrounded by all of these young doctors absorbing by their learned suppositions, I can't help but think about where they were and what they were doing when I was a larval comedian worming my way through the Big Apple in

1980. All of the comics knew and rooted for each other as we sat in the U-shaped alcove at the back of the Comic Strip and watched each other's acts. When you got off stage and rejoined the group, you were given notes on material and gleaned

some new buttons for your act. It was a comedy jam session. Paul Reiser came off the stage one night and announced he'd been cast in a Soap Opera. It was the only soap that went out "Live". He was to play a doctor and had to simply knock and walk into a patient's room. His only line was,

"Well, Mr. Wilson your eyes look much better. You can go home today."

Hey, it's just one line, but the comics choral that it was a great break and great

exposure! Paul reminded us that it was a sweet little paycheck for one day's work.

The afternoon Paul was on the show we all gathered at Bill Maher's apt. in Hell's Kitchen to watch. The show dragged on, and then Paul appeared, white-jacketed and duly concerned about Mr. Wilson. He looked into Wilson's eyes and said, "I don't like the looks of your eyes Mr. Wilson. We'll increase your dosage. I'll be back

tomorrow."

Bravo Paul! You bagged a two-day reoccurring role!

SATURDAY – 8/5/17

Sitting here with a big ol' smile on my face checking Face Book and the outpouring of love, good vibes, prayers, and healing energy. I can feel it all! One of my old friends, whom I believe considers himself to be a Christian, asked me if all of these people sending me healing prayers had renewed my faith in Our Lord and Savior,

Jesus Christ? I wrote back that I consider faith to be a profoundly personal belief in something or someone who's existence cannot be proven. *"Now faith is the substance of things hoped for, the evidence of things not seen."* Hebrews 11:1

I have a diverse community of friends who have faith in different deities within the varietal nooks and crannies of the spiritual realms. If they are sending me energy,

it's because they have faith in energy. Vibes, healing thoughts and, yes, those prayers They all work for me because; residing behind them all there is someone's

deep, abiding faith. It has, actually, renewed my faith in my friends, my community

and the love I feel for them. Got Faith?

What is religion anyway? The doctrine demands, "You must love me, whether you

like it or not. If you don't, I will torture you for the rest of your existence. You are nothing without me. You'll do as I say, or I'll make you sorry." Sounds a lot like an abusive relationship to me. Coincidentally or probably not, because there aren't any, the Cedars Rabbi Guy paid me a visit this afternoon. Is this a good or bad sign? He asked me if I believed in God. I replied that I do, but only if you are spelling it with two o's. I told him that I keep the Goodness of God in my heart and try to treat people in a peaceful god-like fashion. Later I spoke to the folks at the Apple Genius Bar, and they assured me that I'd be able to download the Goodness of God into my Jamie 2.0 heart but it might take some time and I'll need the right cord. Now, where did I put that damn cord? A manana and beyond, Be Nice.

"I like your Christ. I do not like your Christians. Your Christians are so unlike your Christ." – Mahatma Gandhi (A super calloused fragile mystic hexed with halitosis).

On the wall of my room, just to the right of the Sole, I'm scratching off the days, much like the Count of Monte Cristo did when he was vacationing at Chateau d'If. The staff here is so attentive that last night, they woke me three times to ask if I needed a sleeping pill. I had a meeting today with my surgeons Dr. Chung and his team, My Team: Dr. Tang, Dr. Chin, Dr. Chang, Dr. Wang, Dr. Todo and Dr. Kransdorf. I told them that if, and when, they find me compatible Organs, please go easy on the MSG. I guess they through the German doctor in there for diversity. I remember Dick Cavat's joke that he ate at a Chinese-German restaurant and an hour later he was hungry for power. We have a TV channel here that shows *The Jack Benny Show, Burns and Allen*, and *You Bet Your Life*, still funny stuff. One day when the chest x-ray guy, Marvin, stopped by for a dose, I was watching Burns and Allen and asked if he knew who George Burns was? Looking off into the distance, he said,
"Yeah, I think I have heard that name before."
A little FYI and BTW, Cedars-Sinai is at the corner of La Cienega Blvd and George
Burns Drive. I said,
"Seriously, Marvin, you must know who George Burns was."
He hesitated,
"I...I don't think I do. But, then again, I'm not from around here."
Suspecting somewhere like Croatia or Azerbaijan, I queried,
"That's cool, where are you from?"
He flatly answered,
"Orange County."
Aah-ha, that's probably why I couldn't pinpoint the accent!
I did a full-on makeup and wig impression of George Burns on Comedy Break when I was 35. The producer, Molly Miles, thought it was so good that she took it to George's
bungalow next door and showed him. According to Molly he watched the 90 second bit and turning slowly back to her, said,
"The kids good but I'm betta'".

20

MONDAY - 8/7/17

It was a relatively –octopiy entropy free day! Actually, I did get a CT Scan. Before they skewered me with the I.V. of Contrast Fluid. The tech told me that I would feel very warm all over and then I'd feel as if I was peeing myself and wetting the bed but I really wouldn't be…Well, let me tell you…I proved them wrong! Tennis is on T.V tonight. It makes me think of two summers ago when a dear family friend, Brian Klavano, asked if I might consider doing him a favor. He said that he needed some announcers for the Special Olympics World Game which was to be held in Los Angeles on July 25th. I said,

"Of course, Brian, I'd love to help."

I soon learned that one has to be very careful what one agrees to do! Little did I know that I was going to be thrust into an environment of friendly, accepting and smiling, yes ever smiling, volunteers who would soon sweep me up in a week of heart-warming wonderment. I was to be cast as the tennis announcer at the Strauss Stadium on the UCLA campus. I say cast because it was a role. A role I had never played before, yet felt I could have fun with, and boy was I right!! I will always regard the week of July 25th to August 2nd, 2015 as being one of the most wonderful weeks ever! I was met, from the get-go, by great people who were as inspired by the Special Olympians as I soon would become. Walking in from the shuttles every day, there were at least 20 "Good Mornings!" and hugs and fist pumps as I neared the venue. When has that ever happened before? Will it ever happen again?

The childlike behavior of the participants, so full of innocent joy, brought home the childish ways I have behaved in my past and will ever help me keep those moments in check. The week was, in a word, transformational. Case in point, there was a match between Germany and the Netherlands. Germany lost but the player from Germany started dancing and took a victory lap around the court, soon to be tackled and embraced by his Netherlands opponent and as they rolled around the court together, with unbridled joy, it occurred to me that this should be required behavior for the competitors at Wimbledon or, better yet, the clay courts of the French Open. What a divine dust-up that would be! Every person will ever remain in my heart. I must remember to transfer this to the new one. The lesson? You never know when someone asks a favor of you, what a favor they might be doing for you. Thanks, Brian!

The HALLO NURSE! moment of the day was when I was on the phone and a nurse named Destiny appeared at my doorway doing the knock and walk. I said to the person
on the other end,

"Hey A.J. I have to go right now, Destiny's at my door!"

A.J. asked if he could speak with her and I asked,

"Why?"

He said he thought that they should grab some coffee because he'd always wanted to have a date with Destiny. Sleep beckons.

My eldest daughter, Alysse The Elder, hung out with me all day with Lisa Medway, a writer from my T.V. Series in the 80's, Comedy Break. Lisa dropped by bearing crayons and coloring books and a delish salmon/veggie dish. They were both with me when I received the call telling me I'd been moved to status 1-A on the transplant list. This is a good thang. Our Whoops and High Fives attracted some attention in the ward. Bob Robinson brought me some Sushi today because Bob knows that I will be sushi-less for the rest of my days. A Princeton educated rebel, that's just the way Bob rolls. I've known Bob, a true friend, for 40 years, since 1978 when he and his girlfriend, Jeannie, who had been a Breck Hair Model in the 50's, befriended me at the Pier House's Havana Docks bar in Key West. I was doing stand-up there. When Bob worked for Proctor and Gamble, he created Pringles, Perrier, and after leaving P&G, The Pet Rock. Of course, he would be the one to bring me my soon to be Forbidden Fruit.

In 1970's Key West, I had been asked by a resort manager, if I could do two stand up shows on Friday and Saturday nights in their bar? I did, and Bob and Jeannie were in the audience every night! One of our regulars also was Paul Lynde, a tortured closeted gay man of the still socially medieval 70's, who had sought refuge in Key Wasted. Paul and his cronies led by the wonderfully funny Jim McKiernan would find their way to my show, and all hell would break loose. Jim McKiernan and I maintained a friendship long after Paul's death and one night over some Cuervo Gold and that Fine Columbian he told me that, in the 50's, when Paul appeared in a play at The Kenley Players in Columbus, Ohio. Paul told Jim that one of his lifelong dreams was to do stand-up. Jim fished around in the Yellow Pages and learned that the only local club that had comedy in 50's was a bawdy strip club as if there is any other kind, in adjacent Lancaster, Ohio and that they could go over that night after the Kenley performance. They did, and Paul took the stage after the audience had sat through at least six strippers who took

it all off! Paul was introduced and standing meekly at the microphone commented,

"Wow, it smells like pussy in here!"

He took a beat,

"I think!?"

He killed.

I did an impression of Paul in my act…

"I walked into the hardware store and told the salesman I needed a hinge. He said

no problem, you wanna' screw for that hinge? I said no, but I'll blow you for that toaster."When I was silversmith jeweler in Key West, one day Paul walked into my shop on Duval Street, Hi-Ho Silver. As I stood there, star-struck, he pointed to a belt buckle in the case and said,

"Oh, I love that buckle.'

Responding, in his voice, a dream come true for any impressionist, I said,

"I call it my Quick Release."

I proceeded to demonstrate how, if you pushed the stone in the middle, the buckle popped open! He said,

"Oh, I love it! How much?"

"Three hundred fifty dollars, no tax for you Mr. Lynde."

He bought it and for the next five years whenever he found a new boy, which was

fairly frequently, he'd pop his head in the door and say,
  "Jamie, I need a new buckle."
In his voice, I'd respond,
  "Quick release?"
He confirmed,
  "Oh, you betcha!"

WEDNESDAY – 8/9/17

It was a wild night last night! You know how those Tuesday nights can be! Visitors are always a welcome relief from this unceasing tedium but no one had visited me yesterday so I decided to make my own fun. What the hell, worth a try. To kick off my one-man bacchanal, I went full tilt boogie and wheeled my I.V. tree swiftly and rather surreptitiously into my private bathroom. I stood there, hands firmly placed on my hips, weighing the wondrous world of options set out before me. I fixated on the wash basin for a milli-second, as I flashed on an idea and went for it. Scooping up my new vibrating toothbrush I indulged my teeth and gums with the soothingly invigorating bristles. Spiting and rinsing, I was driven to make life on 7% even more exciting so I thrust my I.V. laden arm out snatching a wash cloth from a shining chrome rack. Soaking it in warm water, I encompassed my face with the paper-thin terry cloth touch of my damn near see through hospital washcloth. I languidly stroked on my deodorant, returning it triumphantly into the pink basin that Sarah had cleverly balanced on the side of the lavatory. I put my toothbrush and toothpaste back and wheeled my trusty I.V. tree back to bed. What an adventure I'd had tonight! Best time I've had in weeks! Almost asleep before I hit the pillow, I slumbered peacefully through the requisite bells and dings and pings a hospital brings. I was awoken by a loud clatter. Without 'springing from my bed to see what was the matter', I merely assumed it was a nurse or probably a poltergeist, but I couldn't even open my eyes to say hello. A melatonin and a Norco will do that. The next morning, I went into the bathroom and the pink basin and its contents had been scattered across the floor. Mystery solved. I thought it had been balanced securely on the shelf. How did it fall? Out of the corner of my eye, I saw something move. it was the same sensation that poet Robert Burns must have had as he saw a wee mouse start' awa' sae hasty wi' bickerin brattle. I scanned the room for a mud'rin pattle! Was my poltergeist Trixie, Pixie or King Micky, himself? I slowly shifted my eyes towards the peripheral movement and saw my battery-powered toothbrush wiggling and twitching frantically across the tile floor. Evidently, I had left my poltergeist on all night! God knows what havoc it might have reeked before it finished. So, I sucked it up I bravely grabbed it by the handle steeling myself for the bone-rattling vibration. Happy to say, I shut it down.

24

I forgot to mention that Volunteer Bill came back yesterday and apologized for his first visit, pleading that he had been an engineer. Well, at least that explains the previous "hit by a train" reference. He proposed that he simply viewed things in a very black and white way. He further explained,

"Earlier that day, I had found out that my brother had fallen out of bed and hit his head."

Once again, I succumbed to gratuitous commiseration,

"Oh, my goodness, that's terrible."

"Yeah, now he has a brain hemorrhage, so it's pretty much touch and go. So, how are you doing?"

"Well, I think I was doing pretty great until you showed up…"

"I guess I should leave then."

"You beat me to it, Bill, thanks for bestowing such a positive image upon me."

Trying to lighten things up I said,

"You know Bill, I've got that problem licked, I take an Ambien and a Viagra every night."

Bill was flummoxed enough to ask,

"Why do you do that?"

"Well the Ambien helps me sleep through the night, and the Viagra keeps me from rolling out of bed."

Crickets.

As he turned to leave, Sarah chimed in,

"Wait for a second Bill. I hope you don't mind me asking. When Jamie gets a new heart how will it affect his diabetes?"

"Well I certainly don't mind you asking, but I don't think you're going to like my answer."

Color me surprised!

"I have diabetes, as do many heart failure patients. Once you get your new heart, believe me, your diabetes will get a lot worse, a lot worse."

It was a moment when the true essence of incredulous permeated the room. I brightly
chimed in,

" Go, Bill, just go!"

I just read over Wednesday's entry and was reminded that whenever I use the word lavatory, I think of that night I stayed in a hotel in Pascagoula, Mississippi. I think it was a *Two Seasons* or something like that. I was awoken by a 'drip, drip' only to find a big puddle of water under the base of the lavatory, right next to my bed. I called down to the front desk and said,

"Excuse me sir, but I'm afraid I've got a leak in my sink."

He said,

"Oh, don't worry about it sir, you go right ahead."

Some of the staff at this hospital have taken umbrage to my recent FB posts and have informed me that I will have to take my condition and their treatment thereof a little more seriously. I am in a very germ-controlled environment, where apparently, the germs go primarily to the sickest. Oops, there I go again. I am trying my best to be in compliance with the hospital's regulations. When they change my Schvaanz they require me to wear a mask and I do indeed, wear a mask. It's usually Geoffrey the Giraffe mask from Toys R Us. Hey, I'm just the Tin Man, who am I to argue with The Man or, way worse, incur the wrath of a nurse! I had physical therapy today because I want to be in good shape for the chest crack heard around the ward. I also do it because they make me. Right now, I am beat up…and down for the count!

SATURDAY - 8/12/17

A little doggie I used to love ran into my dreams last night. Her name was *Waffle.* There was a big creek but that's all I remembered when I woke. So, all day they've been measuring my cardiac pressure or something so I had to lay very still. I used the opportunity to try to recapture my fragmented dream. I used to be able to think about a favorite dream and dream it again. Waffle was our little dog in Colorado when I lived with Suzanne. She was Suzanne's dog really. That was quite the life! Our house in Colorado was a hundred and four-year-old two-story wooden Structure, built in 1870. It served as a prototype for just about every scary old wooden house that we've seen in every fright fest from *Psycho* to *The Munster's*. It was actually draftier as well as much more drafty than it looked. Often, we would have to go out for meals because the "gale force" winds in the kitchen were blowing out the gas flames on the range. Leaving that rickety structure, we deftly maneuvered through the speckled grey snow that covered endless frozen ruts carving through the world of mud that was our driveway, a quarter of a mile long, running along the wistful and dry grass strewn base of Archuleta Mesa, framed by the majestic San Juan Rockies. The snow and mud ruts where so deep that winter I couldn't drive my car, a 1950 Lincoln, down the driveway and I had to walk with groceries and whatnot over that rutted half frozen quarter of a mile, daily. What the hell!? It's a little slice of paradise. I was livin' the dream!

On one not so particular day, our neighbor met me on the driveway. The 17-year-old was Danny S, youngest of the Smith Boyz and aimed to walk me to my car. I was certain it wasn't for the camaraderie as he had never offered to carry my books

before. He was the youngest of the Smiths, the oldest family in the valley; they shared our driveway and were trappers of anything that had fur and dared move. Danny, who was quite furry himself but had somehow avoided the family's snares, had 3 brothers and an obese mother. They all smelled, looked and breathed of dry sinew and browned blood. Living halfway up our driveway, we would often get a

glimpse of their house, through curtains of varietal animal pelts tanning in the Colorado sun. The Smiths were mountain people, backward, simple and simply backward. A life-style founded in centuries past. We were the new people, the hippies; unknown critters to these frightened backslid people. If the History Channel had been groveling for programming in those days, the Smiths would have been cable stars! Who were these invaders in their beaded, fringed, jackets? Well, for a start, we were the people with more money and turquoise and silver and pot they could ever imagine. We played loud music, smoked that wacky tobacca, laughed loudly, and sunbathed nekkid on our deck, even in the winter when the sun pierced the softly yielding chill with its glowing, blue sky bright Colorado heat. We were freer and happier than they. Hating us, for all of the above, with a passion born mostly of misconstrued fear, a modicum of curiosity and more than a dash of convoluted envy. You could see it in their eyes, lingering just a hare's breath behind the instinct that was their second, moreover, first nature…killing. It was their love, legacy and their livelihood. So, what was suddenly oh-so-friendly Danny up too? With a vaguely unformed premonition, I suspected that Danny was walking me down OUR driveway because he wanted to show me our dead Alsatian, Canyon. In a flash I thought, are Alsatians actually Armenian because of the -ian? Two weeks ago, our other dog Waffle had come home late at night in a very agitated state. When she jumped up on my lap I found a bullet wound that went into her chest and came out of her back. She was a very resilient Austrialapomoranian Shepard, born from a chance meeting between an Australian Shepard and a Pomeranian. Pity the poor Pomeranian. Anyway, Waffle came home because she could. She had seen the Smiths kill Canyon. I'm reminded that she loved to pass our time together diving for Assorted

Lifesavers in the big creek that ran by our house. By the time she retrieved the fruity treat she was generally at least 50 feet downstream. She didn't like the green ones. So, we would sit there by the river and play a very risky and wet game of fetch with all of the other colors. I ate so many greenies as I watched her flail upstream that, to this day, I can't even smell a green lifesaver.

We had originally gone to Colorado to visit Suzanne's sister, Karin. She was living on a horse ranch with a man named Wolf, who has since changed his name back to James Ward and had a very successful jewelry gallery in Santa Fe. I just looked him up and learned that the gallery is closed and people are chasing him around for owed money and orders. Nonetheless, he is a tremendously talented man. Suzanne and I were invited to stay in the barn above the horses. The nights were cool and the hay was sweet. One day, I told Wolf that I was going into town to look for work.

He said,

"How'd you like to learn silversmith? I could use an apprentice."

A kind gesture to be sure. In the ensuing months, I polished more silver mercury dime beads than you could shake a skin-less finger at. I poured molten silver into inch-by-inch ingots and then pounded them with a two-pound hammer.

The Anglo Silversmiths in Pagosa Springs were an enigmatic group. We would go

to visit the other silversmiths. Most of whom were transplants from California; surfers, and rich kids that liked to ski and get high. We would smoke pot, sometimes taste their mushrooms and always critique and examine their recent bracelets, amulets, or Concho Belts. Rolling their wears slowly around in his hands, admiring the beautiful craftsmanship, Wolf would mutter, 'Ah,ha, Ah-ha, nice work.' Not much more was talked about other than silver prices and who was coming through town and when they might be here. The "who", were mountain men. Handsome, hairy, fringe laden, rich kids from California who were a combination of gem vendors, drug dealers, grocery suppliers and new age traveling salesmen. They might just nail your girlfriend if they stopped by when you

were out of town. They would come to trade supplies for the jewelry you had and sell it to store owners in places like Santa Fe, Taos, Albuquerque, Tucson and Aspen. The silver at the end of the rainbow. They all drove new Toyota Land Cruisers. Wolf and I had some success replicating old style Indian jewelry for the Forrest-Fenn gallery in Santa Fe. A cover article had come out in Arizona Highways magazine, featuring some spectacular examples of Native American Jewelry. Many of the pieces were actually made by Anglos. With the popularity of Turquoise and Silver came greed. The Forrest-Fenn gallery had been ripped off of many, one of a kind, artifacts. So, Wolf and I made replicas for the display cases and the gallery could protect the real stuff in their vaults; putting the smash and grab guys out of business.

So, where was I? Oh, yes. With Danny lifting the rusted and poked hood of an old car to reveal Canyon, our now dead and frozen puppy in the dirty blood-soaked snow. No wonder I digressed I saw Canyon was shot in the hip. "We thought he wus a coyote." Danny said. Canyon probably thought you were a human, I thought. But my head was spinning. Canyon was dead. We were leaving town, taking a business trip to sell jewelry in Tucson. I had been carrying luggage and supplies to the car all morning.

"Didn't leave anything valuable in that their house did ya'?"

Danny casually asked.

The last thing I wanted this half-wit to think was that there was ANYTHING valuable in the house. My mind still reeling from the visual of Canyon frozen dead in the blood-soaked snow, I snapped,

"No, we wouldn't be that stupid."
But we were. We had Navajo rugs on the walls, a Turkish Kilim in the kitchen, my Philco-space-age-TV designed for the opening of Holiday Inns in 1954, several Super Heterodyne radios from the 20's, hundreds of my family slides and 8 mm films from my childhood that I was going to edit into a multimedia show. As I went over the list in my mind, I realized that there was really NOTHING that had any value to Danny and the killer Smiths. There was about $10,000.00 worth of raw sheet silver in the house but I had cleverly wrapped it in brown grocery bags and camouflaged it by taping the bags to the rafters of the attic and texturing the paper with paint, so that, even upon close inspection it would be easily missed. Nobody would ever find it. As we pulled away from the house, I told Suzy that I'd seen Canyon. He was frozen solid and would still be when we returned. We'd bury him when the ground thawed. Suzy cried all the way to Santa Fe where we stopped by a few jewelry stores and had great success selling our wares. By the time we hit Tucson, we had several thousand dollars in our pouches, some beautiful new stones to set and promises of, "make some more, we'll buy as much as you can make." We stayed with some of Suzy's friends at the base of a waterfall canyon, in a beautiful house that was slated to soon become a rehabilitation home for wayward street kids.
One morning, it must have been a Thursday, I was sitting on the commode and I heard the phone ring. A voiced called,
"Suzy, it's your sister."
Huh? Her sister? She lived 20 miles from the nearest phone. What was she doing
calling? I heard Suzy pick up and say,
"Oh my God!"
I opened the door a crack. I called out,
"What happened, Suze, did our house burn down?"
She walked by the slightly opened door and ever so softly and sadly said,
"Yes."
When we got home, we still couldn't drive down the driveway, so we walked, with
Waffle. We reached the car hood, I lifted it up and Canyon was gone. I started to look through the pelts hanging in the sun but stopped when I felt the Smith boys watching us through their carcass curtains. I dropped the hood and tried to look past the pain and confusion in Suzanne's face. Waffle jumped on the car hood. She smelled Canyon. There was pain and confusion in her face too, but easier to look at than Suzanne's. I kept walking and when I reached the plot where the house
had been, I saw a flat black square in the ground. They had burned the house completely down to the ground because they couldn't find the silver. Three weeks
later somebody in Santa Fe showed me a wad of molten silver that had a bracelet,

30

I had been working on, melted to it. They burned it down to find the silver, why hadn't I put that together? The view of the creek was better now, so I walked over and threw in a Life Saver. Waffle just looked at me, unmoving. It must have been a green one.

MONDAY 8/14/17

It was explained to me that all of the precautions they typically take are because when I do receive my new organs, they are afraid of an infection resulting in rejection. I calmly explained that I have been an actor for the last 60 years and by this time I have definitely learned to handle rejection. A couple of days ago, I had a big scare. I experienced a V-Tach. My heartbeat soared to 188 beats per and I passed out. A quick-thinking nurse, who saw me start to go down, swept me into her arms and at that precise millisecond grabbed the Portable Plastic Pee Device I was peeing into, with not a drop on her. She could have been a great defensive end!
Suddenly on a cold metal table I heard my nurse, Jason, shout that infamous Bill Cosby line,
  "I'll get the drugs, you get ready!"
Cresting a sea of dark blue jacketed nurses that roiled around me, a white jacketed Doctor appeared and said, not to my face but directly to my chest,
  "Why didn't you trigger?!"
I asked a nurse,
  "Is he talking to me?"
  "No, he's not sir", she assured me.
  "He's going to have to interrogate your Pacemaker."
It was chaos. In my delirium, all I could imagine was some gumshoe with my Pacemaker under a bright detective's lamp giving it the third degree. So, I loudly interrogated in my best Sam Spade,
  "Exactly where were you on the evening of August 12th, at approximately 6:45 pm? Fine, don't answer me now, just don't try to leave town!"
I garnered some confused looks and earned some knowing nods from the intelligentsia. I've always loved the nodding intelligentsia of the World. I can't be flippant about my condition, I almost died today. I've avoided thinking about my death.
I'm still alive, so I try to think about my life. There'll be plenty of time to think about death, when I'm dead. Other than losing my parents, which is the hardest part of growing up, and a few friends, Death, in large measure, has so far eluded me. There was that time in Colorado when death and killing loomed large. Ever since those wacky Smiths killed one of our dogs, wounded the other, then had the temerity to burn our house down, I've been thinking that I must somehow conjure a means of revenge. I hadn't really felt even a tinge of that vengeful emotion until one day when I was driving back to Buddy and Gail's with a pick-up truck full of groceries. Suddenly I heard the high-pitched b-r-r-r of a dirt bike. Looked over I saw the youngest Smith, Danny, passing me on my left. On his left was a 200-foot precipice. All I had to do was turn my wheel sharply and he would be forced off the side to meet certain death. I looked at him; he looked back and recognized me, frantically looking for his own killer instinct in my eyes. Don't doubt it, it was there but too superficial for me to turn the wheel and force him off the cliff. I must say, it would have been very a very dramatic death because he would have more than likely crashed through the roof of his own house just below, possibly taking out another family member. "Hey Mom! I'm home!" I couldn't kill the kid, I've never believed in instinct, so I chose life. At that moment I devised a fitting revenge. The next day, I ate a dozen of those wax-greasy chocolate covered

mini donuts,
chugged a can of fruit cocktail, and washed it all down with a half a gallon of apple cider. I drove to the beginning of what had been our driveway and walked half way down to the Smiths. Masked by pelts in the windows and bloated by the donuts, sugary fruit and apple juice, I downed a cup of vinegar. Knocking on the door of the Smiths death draped estate. I was delighted when Old Lady Smith answered the door I looked at her fat swollen hands. They didn't seem to have blood on them but I knew they were the hands of a killer and an arsonist. I thought of all the memories she and her boys had taken away from us and before she could close the door, I stick my finger down my throat and threw up. I was aiming for her face but I hit her waist, upper legs and shoes. I've got to work on my aim! She went for her shotgun and I ran knowing full well her aim was better than mine.

TUESDAY 8/15/17

We heard there was a jewelry store available in Silverton Colorado. Silverton was an old mining town that hosted a tourist train every day. The town's population was 750, but when the narrow-gauge railroad came to town, rising 2500 feet through the San Juan's, it carried over 3000 people into town and brought mucho mullah into our store, *Blue Skies Silver*. We actually had no idea what we were doing. We lived in a tent halfway up the mountain with Waffle and my new dog, Spgs. We thought that we could wow them with our stuff. So, I made big stuff, belt buckles and bracelets, and Suzanne made beautiful rings and smaller affordable objects d'arte. After all we had been through, Suzanne and I started to grow apart. A legendary singers daughter came to town and fell in love with my jewelry, I took her to the tent. A leather smith came to town and Suzanne took him to our tent. A recently divorced, New York Lawyer came to town and over some red beer picked me out as her Hippie Cowboy. She got us a room in the Silverton Hotel and suddenly, no one was in the tent. We took our own dogs, worked together but didn't live together anymore. I felt sad.

One day Valerie Perrine came into the store and really flashed on my jewelry. She

told her friend Jill St. John, who owned a store in Aspen about some creations she had seen in Silverton. Simultaneously, our competition, on Main Street Silverton, Harry and Sandi decided that my jewelry had a future and Sandi said, if you're ever in Miami. Give me a call. Suddenly synchronicity went to work. There was one night-club in Silverton, Zhivago's. I had been there before to see the owners wow us with balalaikas. One night, I went into Zhivago's and there was a guest comedian performing, *Ron Maranian, the Armenian Comedian*. He was the funniest man I had ever seen in my life. I related to everything he said, and laughed my heart out, because "my heart" was most affected by his humor. He had a bit about non-violent self-defense where one threw up on one's opponent, stopping them dead in their tracks. It was Kismet. I think that's what happens when you hear something that connects with your spirit, your sense of humor, the joy of your heart.

34

Today they made some changes to my meds by increasing my dosage of Tachrimolodoxypraline and Bayer Baby Aspirin, it was inevitable. Taken together, the side effects include Low Salt Triscuit retention and watching too much Netflix. Believe me, when you're in the hospital and confined to your room, time flies like an extinction of Dodo Birds! I've been here so long that the nurses are starting to become a bit blasé about me. So, sometimes I flat line just to get their attention. Yep, I've been here now for 66 inedible meals and I'm considering a run for Mayor of the Cardiac Pre-Op Unit, so I can hire True Foods to cook for us. Call me a foodie elitist but Scottish Steelhead Smoked Onion Faro, Arugula, Roasted Beets, and a Cilantro Pumpkin Seed Pesto sounds better to me than, Brisket of Beef and Potato Kugel with Twice -Boiled Carrots or even, believe it or not, Diet Jell-O and Raisins.

I was speaking to my Guatemalan nurse about food and I asked if she had ever sampled any of the international cuisine in L.A.? I told her that my favorite international restaurant was Versailles Cuban Food. She effused, in her charming,

broken accent, that she really did 'love these international restaurant'. She said that she always orders the waffles with whipped cream and fruit piled high on the top! As she spun to leave the room, I realized I'd just been Rootin' Tootie Fresh n' Fruitied!

I was thinking today that I'm either going to fly or walk out of this hospital.

For the first time in my life I'm afraid to fly. They say walking is better for you anyway. I concur.

THURSDAY 8/17/17

"It may be that when we no longer know what to do we have come to our real work and that when we no longer know which way to go we have come to our real journey. The mind that is not baffled is not employed. The impeded stream is the one that sings." - Wendell Berry

A dear friend sent this and it resonated with me so much, I had to share this inspired passage with the world. I've come to grips with the fact that for now, Facebook will have to do. I just got a new, rather progressive, Cardio-Resident, Dr. Hamilton, and yesterday after a rigorous exam, she asked if I had any questions? I said,
  "Yes, I do Dr. Hamilton, any chance you can get me tickets?"
Beat.
She exited laughing. I took that as a win. Apparently, she's not one of the Nevis Hamilton's. However, thanks to her, they let me have my first walk today and I did 3 laps around the nurse's station, for a total of 1200 feet, 400 yards, the length of four football fields, 18.1818 chains, and a mere 1.8 furlongs, but hey, it's a start! They've never let a patient, with a Schvannz from the Cardio Pre-Op unit out of their room before, so I'm the Guinea Pig of the Day. Everyone from Doctors, Nurses, to the Maintenance Crew, were ecstatic to see me ambulatory! Geez, one would think I'd just scored 1st place in the Daytona 500! I did a victory lap, fully expecting a champagne salute but all I got was carbonated saline in my I.V.!
Been here for a little over a month now, so to get beyond four walls of my room was a welcome relief. Speaking of welcome reliefs, and I'm sure, I was. I've had a string of fantastic visitors who wisely call before coming up because I could be in a procedure or proceeding to a procedure to which I may have referred to in the preceding sentences. The doctors have limited my visitors to 30 minutes because with less than 10% pumping for me, I tire easily. Once I've been equipped with my 2018 model, they will expand my visits to 6 hours, minimum and, by the way, mandatory! I fear this stipulation may cut down on traffic. You think?

FRIDAY 8/18/17

Every day is full of surprise, delight and inspiration. A typical day starts with being awoken around 5:30 A.M. Hell, I'm up anyway, NOT! Then follows the usual phalanx of painful injections, my favorite is the proverbial Heparin needle to the belly. I think they use 12-gauge galvanized steel tubing, in lieu of a needle most likely to expedite delivery. Heparin is such an effective blood thinner that if I should cavalierly pop a pimple, I could bleed out in minutes. I was delighted to learn that it's extracted from porcine intestinal mucosa. How lovely, intestinal mucous from pigs! I haven't eaten pork for 47 years and I guess this is my reward for sparing all those oinkers? Save your chitlins chillins'. Viva el Chicharron!!!

After being poked and prodded, I fall back to sleep only to be roused by a lovely Philippina who is unbuttoning my shirt and reaching in to adjust my tubing She wraps my arm in a blood pressure cuff and levels my heart, with a level from Home Depot, lining up with my pulmonary pressure tube. This morning when she took

my temp, she said,

"Good, 37 degrees."

I reacted with,

"What, really, 37?"

Lord, save us from Celsius. I promise to convert when I can do the math. After breakfast, I nap until a sweet and burly Guatemalan lady arrives with a pile of towels and a basin of hot soapy anti-bacterial water. During my sponge bath, square pants, I get a momentary glimpse of what heaven must be like. I think it is going to be hot and soapy.

I had a visit from the staff Shrink today. She had two very eager and overly attentive

larval shrinks with her. After some pleasantries she got down to business.

"Mr. Alcroft, I have some standard questions to ask, if you don't mind."

"Of course, fire away," I consented.

"Well Mr. Alcroft the first question is: Have you had any suicidal thoughts?"

My logic snapped to attention, thinking WHAT? Suicidal thoughts!? Suicidal thoughts, why would I be laying in this bed for as long as I have, waiting for a new

heart so that I can have suicidal thoughts? I've been tested for this and stabbed for that. I've been prodded and probed until I have no more places to be violated, why in the name of Christian Bernard would I want to kill myself. Shall I kill myself right now or wait until I receive my life saving organs? Are you out of your fucking mind? What do I have to do to prove that I want to live? But I demurred and said instead,

"Huh, are you kidding me? What's the next question going to be Doctor, how would I kill myself if I wanted to?"

She stumbled, "Well let's skip the next question, shall we?"

"Really? That's disappointing, I was dying to hear it.."

They were smiling when they left.

Everyone will be happy to hear that I've put myself on suicide watch. Other than that it's bidness as usual here, watching and waiting. I feel like I'm in a rerun of M*A*S*H because every time I hear a helicopter take off or land on the roof, I get excited. However, I have to control my excitement, as my congenital condition is adversely affected by adrenaline. I could get so excited when I hear a helicopter land, I could actually die! What's the sense in that? It might be carrying a cooler full of goodies for me and I don't mean a six pack of Hefeweizen and *Green Chile Enchiladas with a mango/pineapple salsa*. I have to chillax. But, my god, I need a little excitement in my life. I have therefore instituted a strict policy with my nurses that they are forbidden from counting, "One, two, three…" before administering any needle, or plastic tubing. They can't even say, "Okay, here we go, ready?" both are verboten! Some of my most well-trained RN's will actually sneak into my room while I'm napping and plunge the needle into my stomach much like the scene in Pulp Fiction where John Travolta trusts an Epi-pen into Uma Thurman's heart, miraculously not puncturing the pericardial sac in her thoracic cavity. My point is, SURPRISE! is all I really have left now. I want to be surprised by injections, surprised when a heart arrives and surprised when I wake up with a new one. I've been warned that sometimes they prep you for a transplant, going as far as to take you to the OP and they actually put you to sleep. When the organs arrive on site, they can decide it's a 'no go' for numerous reasons. Some recipient hopefuls are put to sleep 5 or 6 times before they get their organs! Guess who told me that? You are correct sir! It was Volunteer Bill. My life is fraught with certainty.

SUNDAY 8/20/17

Thank the god of take-out, *Addatipius* and my friends and family who bring me food from the culinary corners of Lower Beverly Hills. A daily task that I do not relish is selecting from the same damn menu day after day, week after week as I circle my selections with my collection of those little, erasure less, four-inch pens. I have so many of them that when I leave here, I could probably open a miniature golf course! Speaking of food, when I have my change of heart, I won't be able to eat certain foods. No RAW cheese, it must be pasteurized or at least past mine. I cannot eat RAW meat, never have had the urge thank you, nor ingest RAW fish, Sushi! When I heard this, I was disappointed and haunted by the prospect that Iwould, never again, be able to delight houseguests with my swallowing a live goldfish, party prank. I will also have to avoid green leafy vegetables and sprouts! That ain't gonna' happen

I continue to conduct Business as usual from my Beverly Hills Office. I take advantage of Pajama Friday every day. My favorite days are Boxer Shorts and Knee Socks Wednesdays and Anti Trump T-Shirt Tuesdays. Oh, they've also told me that I won't be able to drive for a while. When I asked them why, they explained it was because of the air-bag impact. Thank Pirelli that I have a 50-year-old Alfa Romeo! Hey no air-bags baby! I do love to drive that car. If you don't hear from me, I'll be sedated and enjoying a new pumping station in my chest. How happy will I be? I'll be as happy as a baby in a barrel full of tittles!

The people who reach out to me do help my days pass quickly. I was surprised when an old acquaintance, who is now a rabid t-rump supporter, FB'ed me the following, "Jamie, would you accept a heart from a Trump supporter, who has a great, great, great, grandfather, who fighted for the south?" First, I mentally corrected their spelling and grammar, then wrote back, "Come on Tim, it's just an organ. It has no control over who's delusional and addled mind it might be pumping blood into. Like a child born to dysfunctional parents, I shall rise above the challenge. Guess what? If my new heart comes from someone who is left handed
and Norwegian I will not have to relearn English or how to regain the use my right hand! Danke eva' so!

Then there are the delightful calls from old friends, many years and many miles away, like Taffy Danoff from *Starland Vocal Band*. She and her husband, Bill, wrote Country Roads for, or with, John Denver. It is one of the most internationally recorded songs of all time. Learning this, I imagined what it might be like in different languages. Certainly, they would not all refer to West Virginia. In China it might be, "Almost heaven...Hunan Province" or in Germany, "Almost heaven...Baden-Baden", or in Russia, "Almost heaven...Vladivostok" ...Arrrgggh, someone stop me! I'm not even on a morphine drip yet, so I have no excuse! BTW, whomever said "Laughter is the Best Medicine" had apparently never had a morphine drip! Anyway, Bill and Taffy wrote Country Roads when they were Fat City. I think John might have just put his name on it and made it a hit, who knows?! When I was hanging out with Ron Maranian, the Armenian Comedian, he opened for Starland at the Cellar Door in Georgetown. At the end of the week, we had really bonded. I loved their music, *Friends, California Day, Ain't it the Fall?* I especially liked a fun little ditty called *Afternoon Delight*. One night, in the Green Room, over some Cuervo Gold and some Fine Columbian, they told me they had been approached by Denver's label, Windsong, to pick a single from their repertoire. I told them that Afternoon Delight was 'a sure-fire monster hit.' Taffy protested that it was about doing the dirty in the daytime and America would never make something like that a hit. Jimmy Carter was our peanut farming Christian President, Billy Graham was selling out houses of 40,000 followers, America was celebrating the Bicentennial, and *Gumball Rally* was a hit movie. I suggested in the throes of a pretty stoned rant, that the U.S. Treasury had just released a $2.00 bill and only a song like *Afternoon Delight* could help an obviously irrational nation regain its collective composure. It became a #1 Hit and a Gold Record. They were given a network summer replacement T.V. series, four Grammy Nominations and two Grammy's. Where were my lawyers?

TUESDAY 8/22/17

I dreamed about Ron last night. It was a performer's dream where we were in a play with no script or any idea what it was about. Reminds me of the comic at the Just for Laughs Festival in Montréal who came out on stage naked and stood silently in front of the microphone for a full three minutes of his five-minute allotted time before he looked up and flatly said,

"Oh, fuck, not this dream again!"

After the Starland week at The Cellar Door, Ron and I set off for Denver and late on a very dark night somewhere in West Virginia, we traversed a railroad crossing a bit too quickly and the hood, or bonnet, of his MGB, flew off and over our heads, never to be found. Someday an archeologist may unearth it and identify it as a genuine artifact of the British Automobile Scare of the late 20th Century. We detoured to Athens, Ohio where my best friend from High School and College, a master, carpenter, and architect, fashioned a Wood Hood by scoring a fitted piece of plywood and securing it with bolts. Perfect! The only drawback was whenever we checked, and added oil, which was, pretty much, EVERYTIME we stopped for gas, we required a crescent wrench. Hail Britannia! We headed west and somewhere in the Missouri Farmlands the entire electrical system shorted out. I instinctively grabbed the smoking wires from under the M.G.'s open dash. Forty years later I'm still picking copper out of my palms. We were two long hairs in Missouri and knew we had to keep moving! I tried to hitchhike but ended up walking to a nearby town, named Bolivar, smack in the middle of the Lebanon-Pittston-Bolivar Tri-City Area that had a Radio Shack. Returning with a spool of speaker wire, I jerry-rigged the system and we high tailed across tornado-strewn Kansas and got to Denver Ah, the joys of an MGB! Ron was opening for Tom Waits at Ebbet's Field Music Hall. We stayed with Ron's friend Mo Siegel who was focused on his recent launch of a loose tea company he founded in 1969. It was based on his penchant for picking herbs in local Colorado meadows, he called his brand Celestial Seasonings. One night, over some Cuervo Gold and some Fine Columbian we were sitting around Mo's low square, avocado green coffee table, using his teas as chasers. Lamenting the fact that his company was coming up on its 10-year anniversary and the boxes of loose, albeit, delicious, teas were still a tough sell outside of Health Food Stores in Boulder. I suggested, in the throes of a stoned epiphany, that the teas might take off if he offered them in bags; tea bags! The epiphany was mutual. At first, he put the tea in hand-sewn muslin bags because paper tea bags were too establishment, and, dare I say, more natural. Soon they opted for the paper bags and made deals with Kraft, The Hain Food Group, Trader Joe's, Sprouts and the tour of their factory now attracts over a million people a year. Cue the lawyers! Hello?

WEDNESDAY 8/23/17

This will have become a three-night rant, so now we'll go back to Key West, where I became best friends with brilliant film producer and exotic herb importer, B.J. Martin. His wife was a flower/rainbow child named Sunshine. She was the owner of the Art House Film Theatre that featured husband B.J.'s Key West Picture Show midnight showings of the *Rocky Horror Picture Show, Flesh Gordon, That Obscure Object of Desire, Seven Beauties*, and like-minded Art Films. Sunshine was the mother of two and when B.J. eventually went to a federal prison in Texas for three years because he wouldn't snitch on his import minions; he protected his mules by doing hard time. Sunshine was named Mother of the Year by the City Council, ah, Key West! Both B.J. and Sunshine were close friends with Jimmy Buffet, from his early days of playing at the Half Shell Raw Bar. With B.J. in the clink, Sunshine needed a job so with Jimmy's backing, she started up the Margaretville Restaurant on Key West's Duval Street. After Mack and I had become a Comedy Team in 1980, Mack and Jamie did four SOLD OUT shows there. One night, after a show, over some Cuervo Gold and some Fine Columbian, sitting around B.J. and Sun's pool, I asked her how many Margaritas' they sold at the shows. She said that they had sold thousands. Once again, without my lawyers anywhere in sight, I suggested that she should consider launching a line of Jimmy Buffet Tequila and Margarita Mix with a series of like branded lost shakers of salt. They now have 9 Resorts, 32 Restaurants, 3 Casinos, a series of Retirement Communities. Still NO LOST SHAKER OF SALT! I guess I should keep my stoned epiphanies between my lawyers and myself!

THURSDAY 8/24/17

"One day we will look back on this and laugh." When I came across this quote, on a Hallmark Card I received from my cousin Patty, I remembered that it was originally said by Publius Vergilius Maro (Oct 5th 70 B.C.). Also known as Virgil, a classical Roman poet, best known for three brilliant works, the Bucolics, the Georgics, and the Aeneid. He was the son of a farmer in northern Italy and came to be regarded as one of Rome's most celebrated poets; his Aeneid is still considered Rome's national epic. Or perhaps it was renowned public irritant Vergil Bubba Earl Shoefelter? Also known as Blackout Bubba (Aug. 20, 1951 A.D.), a classic town drunk, best known for the night he shouted racial epithets at himself until a fight broke out amongst himself leading to eviction from the local Optimists Club. He was summarily convicted of pissing off the Sherriff, absent of a jury of his peers, because no one was quite like him. The illegitimate son of a Snap-On-Tool salesman, he was from southwurstern Illinois and came to be regarded as the go to guy for putting the kibosh on any local function, by merely schlepping through the door. His adenoidal tone, when singing inebriated was considered, by most, to be the Tri-County's most annoying public nuisance. I might be going out on a limb here, but my guess is it was the former Virg who indeed said, 'One day we will look back on this and laugh.' To which I say, why wait? Let's laugh now!I must say that being sequestered on the same floor of a multi-story building is pushing me over the edge of ornery. For instance, the nurses, who have 12-hour shifts, pass the syringe at 7 p.m. That's right, Jeopardy 7 p.m.! What the Hell?! They start sharing information about me, comparing my numbers and my condition standing at monitors on either side of the room, as I persist in watching my show. The new shift nurse, whom I've never met, asked the other nurse,

"What is he doing?"

She was asking why I was shouting random questions at the T.V.

"WHEN WAS THE BATTLE OF HASTINGS?",

"WHO WAS EURIPIDES?",

"WHAT WAS MARTHA AND THE VANDELLAS FIRST HIT?"

Stuff like that. I felt compelled to explain that, instead of going back to college for a doctorate, I'd chosen to watch Jeopardy religiously. However, I am aware that Watching Jeopardy is considered, in some circles, to be an affliction of the elderly. I wanted to say,

"So, put a cork in it!"

But I deferred, adding,

"Hey gals, want to watch Wheel! with me?

Tonight, my nurse told me that she had once been a master sergeant in the U.S. Army. By the end of the night, I wanted to assure her she had not lost her falsehearted caring and genuinely abusive touch. She started by giving me my injections like she was back in the Non-Com Bar playing darts, inflicting an equivalent degree of bulls-eye pain. As her face remained tranquil, but I know she was saying, 'Come on Soldier, suck it up!' Suddenly her *Reveille* phone ring distracted her and as she reached to answer, she inadvertently twisted and erratically changed the angle of the needle. I grimaced from head to toe. I assumed she must have been thinking, 'Hell, I've administered to quadruple amputees who've complained less than you!' At least that's what I hear. In actuality she's probably just thinking, "is that my phone ringing or is someone flatlining? These 12-hour shifts are hell, god I miss boot camp!'

The HALLO NURSE moment of the day - This morning I was sitting yoga-style on my
bed, chanting, "New Day, New Heart, New Day, New Heart. "When a Lab Tech came in to give me a chest X-ray. He said,
"Good Morning Mr. Alcroft, can I interrupt you for a minute?"
I took the initiative to acquiesce to the inevitability of interruptions in everyday life and
said,
"Sure."
As he set up, he queried,
"What were you doing there?"
I responded,
"Have you ever heard of a Mantra?"
"Sure have! My sister drove one for years…a red convertible, she loved it!"
I was glad she loved her car. I love cars and missed driving every day. Then he placed a lead blanket over my tapped out reproductives, and I caught myself wondering exactly how long that lead blanket had been leaking on him? He had a hard time getting the excellent picture, he needed, finally asking,
"Jeez, man, are you a runner?"
"No, but I do enjoy competitive sauntering."
"Excuse me for saying so but you have very large and long lungs!"
"Thank you."
Now I'm thinking, damn! I wish I'd have known that when I was single. It would have been a great opening line at parties.
"Hi there, my name is Jamie. I've been told I have very large and long lungs. Want to go outside and catch some air?"
Breathe deeply the gathering storm and when you take a deep breath, hit you back tomorrow.

SATURDAY 8/26/17

I've decided that when I eventually get my previously enjoyed heart, I'm going to take action with an existing Donor Promotion group or even form a non-profit of my own. Something like Have a Heart, or Give of Yourself, or Liver Let Die might be good. Or for ocular donors I'll Keep an Eye Out 4 You, perhaps You Ain't Gonna' Need These Where You're Going, or Take my Organs, Please, might work too. Oh, one more still in the running, Why Aorta! The statics are grim. In the USA alone 20 people die every day because their needed organ isn't available. As I wait and wait, I'm learning that the U.S. stands only mid-way among developed nations with Organ Donors at about 53%. Spain leads the world at about 68%. Not all countries require that people register as organ donors at the D.M.V. or online as we do. Spain and others have opt-out systems in which citizens are presumed organ donors and killers of the road, unless they formally opt out. Australia has created a Donor Leave program, much like maternity leave. Other countries even offer incentives such as preferred treatment for donors, if they should need to become a transplant recipient. Hello! That's me! Let's look at the numbers. Each human can donate 27 usable items, saving and enhancing the lives of the hopefuls. Man, that's some humanitarian recycling! Oddly enough, there is a lot of blowback from people when it comes to becoming donors. They think they might need their bodies in heaven? Where will they put their wings? The other fear is that, because there is such an organ shortage, their vitals will be harvested before they are dead. I realize I'm going to need some leverage. The incentive for potential donors is so simple. If you sign up as a donor and you should you ever need and organ, an eye, some skin or a face, you get moved to the top of the list. 27 organs, no waiting! If I can speak to a group of, say, 500 and, after being charmed by my discourse just 3% decide to become donors – that's 15 donor's times 27. So, 405 people will be able to benefit, or dare I say live, because of the kindness of strangers. Dead strangers but strangers no more. Speaking of numbers, this morning I said to my nurse, in a somewhat disheartened tone,

"Well, Kristina (sigh), today is day number 38."
To which she cheerily responded,
"Yes, it is Jamie, isn't that great! Number 38, one-day closer!"
Brightened my day! She was so right. One day closer to the unknown.
More palaver anon.

SUNDAY 8/27/17

After hearing from Taffy, the other day, it seems that the world of music is embracing me. Another hint of that harmonious vortex was today when I received a totally unexpected and inspirational note from Russell Hitchcock of Air Supply. He had been made aware of my congenital circumstance by promoter and friend, Jerry Stanley and Russell's manager, Steve Levesque. It read:

Hey Jamie, Russell from Air Supply here ... hoping you get to the top of the list ASAP and that you have a successful surgery and a speedy recovery!! Just remember the lyrics from Making Love Out of Nothing at All - "My heart is a drum, and it's lost, and it's looking for a rhythm like you. You can take the darkness from the pit of the night and turn into a beacon burning endlessly bright" Take good care mate. Peace & Love, Russell Hitchcock.

BTW, Mack and I opened for Air Supply a scant 27 years ago! I'm chuffed to say that I've been penning a song myself and will dedicate it to all of my dear friends and my treasured family. It's a country-western ditty called "Darlin', Even Though I've had a Change of Heart, I'm Still Gonna' Love You." Today was my 33th day in a small room, in a big building, waiting for a huge miracle. Generally, if I were celebrating a day somewhere, I would be wondering, 'What can I do today? Where can I go to celebrate?' Well, I have made some exciting plans that I'd love to share with you! I will be wheeling my I.V. tree over to the window to watch the tops of people's heads and try to identify who is wearing a Joseph Banks, buy one-get-two free, suit. I also plan on weaving my 20+ feet of tubing into a lanyard for my latch-key. After that, I have plans to recruit Lucretia "The Scrubber" Reyes for what I like to call my Sponge Bath Square-Pants. You can't beat unbearably hot water and anti-bacterial soap vigorously applied in a Squidward direction. A ritual that I shall miss until my first hot shower, in about three months or so, or so they've promised! These 33 days have yielded 66 visitors. I have no idea who some of them are but I've learned that the weird thing about being in a hospital is that EVERYONE knows where to find you. One of my visitors began commiserating with me about my impending pain as he was currently undergoing treatment for tennis elbow! Moments like that make me count my blessings. Thank God for just a little bout of heart failure, right?

MONDAY 8/28/17

I must say, I am flat out aghast at how much plastic they use and abuse here, without any 21st or even 20th century epiphanies regarding recycling. It's ridonkulous, as my

daughter Alysse would say. So, I have put into motion my own personal war on Styrofoam. (A tip of the hat to *Foam World* in Philly). One of my innovative blows, for the environment, is to have the nurses place my pills in a P.R.P.C. (Perpetually Recycled Paper Cup) which has so far endured many med administrations in 40 days. BTW, that figure 40 should not be taken lightly. It represents 80 Heparin shots to the belly and believe me, at this point my stomach is shot from those shots! Speaking of meds, as I was attempting to do, they are trying to bring my pulmonary pressure down to acceptable levels. It has been explained that if my pressure is too high when they cut me open, I'll explode and ruin the drapes.

They change my meds daily. A recent addition to my vastly expanding regimen is Sildenafil, a first cousin of Viagra, which is injected directly into my mouth. At first blush, I thought they were giving me this Viagra derivate to prevent me from rolling out of bed. Remember that joke?

Last night, I was getting my nightly phalanx of meds from a new nurse. She methodically poured my pills into my hand and with typical panache as I slammed them down with my water chaser. I sighed, and she said,

"Oh wait, one more!"

Handing me the PRPC… without hesitation, I poured what I thought were my remaining pills into my hand only to find that it was the liquid Viagra. She was expecting me to drink it! Instead, it was dripping through my fingers, so we wiped it off and as she reached for another dose, she squirted in this time, as she squeezed open my mouth. No harm, no foul – but it's odd, I haven't been able to bend my fingers all morning! Expecting the typically turgid tongue, I am now experiencing chronic Phallic Phingers. Go finger?

TUESDAY 8/29/17

I've been speaking on the phone to a lot to of friends near and far. Yesterday, I heard from my former William Morris agent, the legendary Jeff Witjas, who has become a great friend. He told me, in no uncertain terms, if I was looking for a heart, I was barking up the wrong tree because agents don't have them! Then he told me that if, by some miracle he helped me find a heart, he wanted 10%. We always have a few good laughs, a great guy!

I sprang an Old Chestnut on the surgical team yesterday when they asked me if I had regular bowel movements. I told them that yes, I was. In fact, I am so regular that I go every morning, like clockwork, at 7:30 A.M. but there was a problem. They looked concerned and said that my regularity was a good thing. I agreed that a regular 7:30 A.M. movement was good, but the problem was that I don't get out of bed until 8:15 A.M. Once they huddled over whether it was a joke or not, they told me that I would be able to see a photo of my old heart once it has been replaced. It reminded me too much of when your mechanic brings out the greasy, corroded fuel pump that he replaced, to prove that he put in a new one! Right?

The owner of the The Ice House, Bob Fisher, stopped by today and noticed the beautiful orchids by my window. We discussed how difficult it was to keep them alive and he disclosed that he had been given some beautiful, fully bloomed, orchids and with a judiciously measured application of water had kept them thriving for over a year. One day when he was carefully watering them with an eye-dropper, his assistant walked in and asked,

"What the hell are you doing?"

He turned to her, as she said,

"Those are plastic! (Beat) But you have done a beautiful job keeping them alive."

I hoped that my transplant team is blessed with similar skills!

WEDNESDAY 8/30/17

From the minute I was told that my only way to live longer was to find a new heart. I held out hope. Knowing someone would have to die for me to live is a sobering thought. No, it's not, it's an unfuckingbelievably shocking thought. Right now I have no interest in meeting with or reaching out, in any way, to the family or friends of my forever to remain anonymous donor. That might change but I was told by a therapist who I hadn't seen, or slept with, in over 40 years, that this type of relationship could become fraught with peril. Imagine (if you will) I was invited to a family picnic where everyone could meet the guy who got Bryan's heart? That's Bryan with a Y.
  "Jamie, it is Jamie, isn't it? Is that short for James?"
  "Yes, it is."
Soto Voce gasp.
  "Bryan's middle name was James."
    "Oh wow!"
I exclaimed, acquiescing that James might have been an uncommon name, perhaps in the Ming Dynasty.
  "Ah...Jamie, would you like some Potato Salad?"
  "Sure, thanks."
I dug into the potato salad, eating around the bits of celery.
  "Oh my god Marlene look at that would you!"
To me,
  "We used to have to pick the celery out of Aunt Sophie's Potato Salad for Bryan. The
  boy just couldn't eat celery."
I immediately ate my celery.
There is something about being the 'New Bryan' I'm not completely comfortable with.
I can't imagine that Bryan did stand-up, played tennis, skied, was a silversmith, a DJ or was totally into cars but I can hear it now,
  "Oh, Bryan loved his cars didn't he Marlene?"

THURSDAY 8/31/17

For those of you uninitiated healthy and lucky people out there. There is no such thing as modesty in a hospital. Your package is no longer yours and peeing modesty goes right out the window. I know what you're thinking but don't even go there. Anyway, the windows don't open. It's time for HALLO NURSE! One of mine dropped a true gem today. I was scheduled to move out of the Motel 6 ICU room at the St. Regis and my ICU nurse fluttered in and threw away,

"So, I hear we're going to lose you today!"

Her unfortunate choice of words took the fun out of leaving. Have semantics become

a thing of the past? As I write, the emergency beepers on two of my I.V.'s have been going off. After two months of listening to these monitors beeping, I will never be able

to hear another truck back up without a cardio flashback! I am so ready for this new heart; I wish I could just pick one out of the air. As I overheard a gas station attendant

in Arkansas once say as a comely customer passed by, 'I would if I could but I cain't so I ain't.'

Be Well, Stay Well, and Love Magnificently. Your Trusty, not yet rusty, Tin Man.

50

I've had a SECOND Swan-Ganz implanted in my neck today! As I mentioned it delivers meds directly to the old ticker. The first one was so uncomfortable; I made a point of blinking away the tears complained frequently enough, and for long enough, to as many people as I could find within the confined space to which I have been assigned. Yes, they were mostly staff but I thought that if I had any chance with anybody, it would be them! The angel on my left shoulder was telling me to live with the pain, 'hell, you're getting heart and a liver fir gads sake!' Just as the angel on my right shoulder was warning me that they would have to take the old one out to be able to put the new one in? The same vein!? No way. Would that there could be another

vein? Well, an hour later they took it out and put the new one in. Thank any and all of the acknowledged deities and those hidden from us, I know you're out there. They found another VEIN! The second coming of the Schvannz is, so far, much more comfortable considering I have a tube in my neck that goes into my heart. I wonder why there is always more pain at night, well there is. Are they giving me more meds or fewer? Perhaps I need more. I don't think I'm getting enough and why should I live with any pain anyway, how much am I paying for this room. It occurred to me to call the Front Desk but the last time I did that, I ended up peeing in the sink. As we all learned in grade school, the Swan-Ganz catheter was developed by Dr. Swan and his trusty collaborateur, Le Marquis de Ganz. It was my surgeon who told me this saga as he was twisting in the Ganz part. After receiving this little tidbit of medical dirt, I broached to my surgeon,

"Doctor, this IS a Jewish Hospital, right?"

"Yes, Mr. Alcroft, it is. Why do you ask?"

"Well with that affiliation, I doubt if I'm getting a Swan-Ganz. I'll more than likely be getting a Schvannz-Gantz!" (in my best Billy Crystal, old Jew) I added, "How's the Schvannz, fresh today? How fresh, let me see it!! I'd like it sliced very thin, as a matter

of fact, slice it really thin and when you've done so...slice it again!" At this point, I have about 7 of my 12, medical team, calling it my Schvannz...which, can turn the heads, of the uninitiated, in the hallways. My standard greeting is,

"Good Morning Doctor."

They hit me back with,

"Good morning Jamie. How's your Schvannz?"

"Can't complain, yours?"

I love it!!! They are so easy to train.

SATURDAY 9/2/17

I was brutally awoken by my overhead fluorescent light that I call The Marquee.
I heard a fleeting,
  "Whoops" emitted by my nurse, Mia Paramujibar, and then an apologetic,
  "Good Morning Mr. Alcroft."
When it's turned on, it's like sleeping at the foot of the NUART ticket booth. It's been years since any of us have done that, right? Right? Can I have a show of hands? I'm still in the ICU because there are certain thermo-nuclear drugs being administered that apparently can't be dripped in the other wards. I have no idea what they are, nor what they do. I like it that way. Just save my life. I miss the sixth floor, it was like the
St. Regis in Osaka, compared to the ICU-6. I had one of those experiences that one should have only in a hospital. In my first eleven days her I became constipated,
impacted, obstructed and pretty damn miserable. They gave me one of those magical
ass rockets and I was finally but relieved but In the process I gave myself a self-inflicted episiotomy by delivering a small watermelon. I haven't decided on a name yet. A nurse, Evelyn Cho, came in and took a look at my recent birth canal.
Fortunately, I required no stitches but here's the kicker. I did not see Evelyn Cho until
52 days later when they sent me back to this ICU. She came into my room to swab my nostrils and then she said,
  "My name is Evelyn, and I'll have to swab your rectum as well, so just lay on your
  left side please."
As I did, and she set about swabbing, she exclaimed,
  "Oh, wait a minute, I remember you!"
Must have been my smirk.

SUNDAY 9/3/17

"oil, oil, OIL…." Were the first words Dorothy heard from the clenched jaw of that rusty, funnel headed fellow in the shiny tin barrel. Right now, I'd have to agree with him. Fluids, of any color or viscosity, would be extremely welcome in this increasingly eroded body. I have lost over 45 lbs. (23 Celsius) of fluids, since being admitted to

Casa Cedars. I'm thirsty all of the time; however, it has thankfully put me in touch with

my feminine side, who I've always liked hangin' with. I know I'm more in touch because, since losing all of that weight, I'm anxious to get home and see what I fit into. If I keep thinking this way, they've threatened to put me on a Testastallone drip! I would be remiss, (or is it reMs.?) if I didn't take a moment to thank my dearest Sarah, our rough and ready children, Alysse, Hayley, Thatcher, and their friends, William, Arielle, Jack Mullins, Lauren Dubac, Bietak Productions, Sylvia Froescher, Matt Kessinger, Dina Carruthers, Jaki and Nigel Carroll for their help moving us from an overstuffed apartment in Thousand Oaks to a freshly overstuffed apartment in Valley Village. Odd that we lived, and brought up our children, in Westlake Village, are now in Valley Village and neither one remotely resembles a village! Of course, neither does The Village in NYC. I Love L.A. (no, I do!) 'It takes a village is attributed to Hillary Rodham Clinton from her book It Takes a Village and Other Lessons Our Children Teach Us. Would that she had been prescient enough to realize that it also takes an Electoral College.

Being here now for 46 days, many have suggested that I must be at my wit's end and I very well might be, but I can't remember where they began. They also ask why I'm about to put myself through this? As dear friend and sage B.J. Martin told me last week, 'Remember Jamie, you can't walk on water unless you get out of the boat.' That is a great piece of advice that B.J. gave me. Hey, I'll take whatever I can get, right? I'm hoping beyond hope that for me, 2017 will be the Year of Giving. Also hoping that I can be a "slam bam thank you mam" happy camper by Christmas; three months away. Christmas and the Holidays are most associated with giving. Unless you are under 18, then it's all about getting. I remember being excited last Christmas, because I knew what I was going to get for everyone! It was like looking at a box of chocolates

and knowing precisely which piece had your favorite filling. It was a beautiful warm day, so I put the top down, as I went to the mall in my mint condition 1966 Alfa Romeo Duetto. I was ready to shop 'til I dropped. At that time of year, trying to find a parking spot was like trying to find a Mensa Club member at a Trump rally. Wait! There's a lady laden with shopping bags limping to her car under the weight of giving! So, I followed her and slowly pulled up to the side with my turn signal blinking my intentions. Patiently waiting for her to load her loot, she gave me a knowing smile and a nod as she climbed in her car. She put her foot on her brake, giving me false hope. Then she proceeded to plug in her phone, check her messages, after adjusting her rearview and side mirrors, and saw to every personal issue other than shaving her legs. Suddenly, her back up lights glowed with new hope. She carefully inched out of her spot. I gave her a wide berth. As she pulled out and away, an overly anxious shopper, in a BMW M3, whipped around the corner and slid into the spot. My Gut reaction was to rear end the S.O.B., but my more genteel instincts enveloped me with the spirit of the season. I put the Alfa into first and started inching away to find another spot, no worries. A young man energetically bounded from the M3, obviously oblivious to what had just transpired. He proceeded to say the words guaranteed to incur the wrath of any Alfa owner,

"Hey, is that one of those Fiats?"

Blinded by disbelief and aghast at his ignorance I applied the clutch and braked to a halt. Leaning out, I educated him on multiple levels. "Actually, it's an Alfa Romeo," I offered, proffering,

"And, it's fifty years old." Adding, "You probably didn't notice that I've been sitting here, with my turn signal on, for at least ten minutes, waiting for that spot you just stole from me."

He called my car a 'Fiat' (Fix It Again Tony), and now he was suffering the slings and arrows of my Alfisti wrath! I'd had enough, shaking my head I released the clutch and pulled away, as he wryly commented,

"Fuck you and your old fuckin' Fiat, old man."

My biting retort was to smile and say,

"Well, Merry Christmas to you too."

To which he merrily called out,

"Shove it up your wrinkled old ass."

I circled the lot a few times and found a perfect spot in the shade of a tree. I exhaled my frustration, trying to let the incident dissipate. Got some great stuff for the family and had a few laughs with the salespeople. As I returned to my treasured spot in the shade I passed by The Cheesecake Factory, filled with customers enjoying a sunny California pre-Christmas lunch. At the last table sat Mr. M3, sipping on Pink Lemonade, with two girls. I passed by unnoticed. Walking towards my car, I happened to pass by his Beemer in the "stolen spot." It occurred to me to leave him a Christmas card. I wrote:

Dear Mr. Beemer – I hope you had a pleasant lunch with your two lovely friends. I wanted to share with you how glad I am I took that part-time-holiday job at the Cheesecake Factory. Had I not taken that job I would have missed my opportunity to urinate in your Pink Lemonade. I take great comfort in knowing that for the rest of your life you'll remember me for this gesture of giving. I sincerely hope that those two lovely innocents, you lunched with, didn't kiss you 'goodbye' on the lips. Once again have a Merry Christmas. Ain't that a pisser? That old fuckin' guy in the Fiat.

When I walk the hallways, I always wear my Pajamas so I've become known as *The Pajama-Guy*. Maybe it's the other way around? I think that will be a good pen-name someday, *Guy Pajama*. With a name like that I could pull off a paisley cravat and perhaps a satin smoking jacket....too much? These "Hospital Gowns" that the 'Hall Zombies" wear, without shame, or underwear, are a joke! It's like a clothing optional beach where you are constantly asking people to, "Please cover up!". The 'Gowns" as they so munificently call them, are not only the farthest garment from a gown imaginable, but they are also unattractive, uncomfortable, un-wearable and all of the UN's known to man! Everything about them is uncomfortable. Kind of a ONE SIZE FITS NONE.

I tell you what; if I were runnin' this joint, I would institute a policy that all patients admitted to the Heart Transplant Unit, be shaved entirely before encountering any of those E.K.G.'s or nipple & snap sensors, some the are size of a Personal Pizza. When ripped from the skin, they remove the follicle equivalent of a Ken Doll's head of hair. I call them my "Alabama Brazilian's." They are not very big on Local Anesthetics around these parts, which I'm sure cost a pretty penny, because we're so close to Beverly Hills and Hancock Park?! I love, not, the way they will say, 'This MAY hurt a bit, which means it really WILL!' or, 'You're going to feel a little pressure' followed by a SHARP PAIN! I am still trying to co-operate and toe the line as much as I can. Yesterday my unit head, Dr. Hage, 'call me Tony,' asked if he could use me to demonstrate my treatments and their effect on my tubing interstate, which actually does date back to the Eisenhower Administration. I agreed, "Of course you can." Adding, "In fact, one of my ancestors was a cadaver for "Grey's Anatomy." From the middle of the cluster, someone said,

"I love that show!"

Ah Millennials, can't live with them, can't live with them! I wonder if *Grey's* is still in print?

Today a nurse brought me a bottle of Perrier. I find it much easier to swallow the phalanx of meds they give me every ten minutes with a bit of the bubbly, preferably in a bottle. It washes the gathering hordes down my throat. I slipped her $10 and she pleaded with me not to tell ANYBODY, not about the ten-spot, but about the contraband sparkling water. She trusted me with a secret. I was 11 when I was told my first colossal secret by my parents. Made even more thrilling by virtue of the fact that it was the very first incredible secret I had ever been asked to keep. Oh, my wee Scots grandmother had told me about the old couple who went into town and the wife turned to the husband and said; Sweetheart, I'm going to go to the A&P.' He said. 'Okay then darlin', I'll go to the Y. & shit.' She asked that I never tell anyone she had told me that joke but, at 8, I didn't regard it as a secret so much as I considered it material. On the other hand, the secret my parents told me was sacred. It was the first time I'd savored how delicious a secret could be. Lying in my cozy single bed in 1959, drifting off and imagining the bright moment in the future when the secret could be disclosed to all. Isn't the best part about a secret the anticipation of when it can be given away, plotting who the first recipient will be and when the inevitable disclosure might take place! I could hear Grandma in the next room crying, she must have known the secret too. During the day, she sat in her perch by the upstairs window chain smoking Viceroys and popping nitroglycerin pills like popcorn. She was watching a movie no one else could see; too impossible to ever be made. It was out-takes of her life with my grandfather, four years dead; movies playing on a loop because she never wanted to change the reel. When I would catch her eyes, as I rounded the top of the stairway, knowing full-well that she was lost in her private screening, she denied my gaze; knowing I knew about her movie, maybe even the secret. Someone once said, 'Never give up and never borrow sorrow from tomorrow'. Something she would never know, as I would never know what had cursed me with what was forever to be known as My Black Thursdays. Was I alone the dark perpetrator of those three inconceivable Thursdays? Why did this happen then and now again? I couldn't cease the momentum or stop the events. The first Thursday started out like any other day before any other Friday. I went to school and like every other fifth grade day I got sucked into the spiraling vortex known as Julie Kennedy. It was an elementary E-Ticket to hell. Mrs. Kennedy had those angry high-heel shoes that you could hear clicking down the hallway, from the next school district. She had a temper and a vengeance that by the end of the year had taken a patch of hair from the back of my head the size of a Portobello mushroom. She had never actually, physically touched me. I simply became a member of Judy Kennedy's exclusive clique, the 4 A's, the Advanced Alopecia Anxiety Academy. As I said, the first Thursday began, like, but then ended unlike, any other. The carpenters finished up while I was at school and the new leather furniture was just arriving as I got off the school bus. I debussed, 'Stopped, Looked and Listened.' My mother gave my sisters and me milk and chocolate-covered grahams. Elementary school homework had yet to be thrust upon children in the late fifties, so we played with our dog and friends. With precision timing, I made my eleven-year-old excuses and entered the house surveying the newly completed family room. I told Mom that the girls were fighting outside, and she set out to settle the alleged dispute. I had estimated my chances that they would be fighting to be about 98%. There was still a late winter chill in the air that hadn't left the family room. As I entered the space, I was greeted by the smells of new carpet, leather, and freshly varnished wood. My parents had bought a small electric space heater to warm the, under-construction, but now new family room. To quell the chill and neutralize the conflicting fragrances, I plugged in the space heater and left it glowing in the midst of all the newness. My timing was perfect for as Mom returned with my bickering sisters in tow, we were simultaneously distracted by the sound of Dad's '59 Chevy Impala's tires crunching the driveway gravel between their fresh new treads. My young sisters and very young Mom moved, transfixed by the sound, toward the front door. With one swift motion, I swept the space heater to the side of the couch. Moving fluidly into the aluminum and Formica maze that was our kitchen, I proceeding with my daily chore. I mixed two Seagram's and waters on lots of rocks, for my folks whom I anticipated, would welcome the opportunity to sip their cocktails in the warmth of our new family room. Dad was greeted at the door by his loving girls and as we all walked toward our new family room, the gathering aromas of new carpet, leather, and freshly painted new wood, now were joined by an unfamiliar smell, of burning flesh---but more pungent, rawer and stinging. I cringed at the sight of the space heater burning a neat pattern of coils into the side of the new couch. Like an Apollo thruster, an explosion of flame and light burst from the charred brown leather. It occurred to me that there hadn't been a space program in the family room earlier, as the drinks were thrown against the angry flames, quenching them minimally, though still managing to get enough splash-back from the dousing to short out the electric heater and sizzle a few major fuses that were loudly popping in the basement like the muzzle loaded cannons at the end of the 1812. In retrospect, they rather symphonically added a touch of class to the chaos. That was the first Thursday of the trilogy but by far not the blackest, or, should I say the most black?

SUNDAY 9/3/17

In the days of endless family dinners, devoid of conversation, which followed, I harbored a modicum of dignity, silently attested to by the fact that I remained in possession of the secret. It was a delicate flower to cling too. I was living in early onset adolescent terror. Weeks passed, and I'd been doing my chores with extra attention to the detail of perfection in their execution. It was fall and all of those glorious boughs not so long ago laden with lush green leaves, providing the much welcome shade from the sweltering Ohio summers, were now surrendering their brittle brown foliage blanketing the immaculately groomed neighborhood lawns. Dad had bought one of the newest devices meant to replace the ordinary rake, a 50's precursor to the BR-
BR-APPING, deafening, Mexican leaf blower that has apparently replaced the broom,
at least in California. This contraption was a leaf sweeper with a stiff, brown bristle
roller and a large canvas catch bag for those thousands of dryly departed mementos
of summer. I knew that I probably had to mow the lawn one last time but it was now covered with a leafy comforter. So, I commandeered the Sears Super Deluxe Leaf Sweeper out of the garage and set about cleaning the lawn. As was the style of the era, before the GOP went into denial about Global Warming, the leaves fluttered effortlessly into the canvas catcher until it was brimming over and I piled them in the gutter between the strip of grass beyond the sidewalk and the road. Also, in keeping with the oblivious observances at the turn of that deluded decade, I set them afire and returned to my sweeping to secure more tinder for the sweetly burning blaze. I repeated this process several times and as I was delivering the fifth or sixth load to the blazing roadside incinerator, my mom called from the front door that I had a phone call. A phone call, at eleven years of age, was akin to receiving a telegram at the turn of the century or having a breathless centurion run up with a wax-sealed message from a ruling Caesar. I was full of anticipation as to whose voice might surprise me from the other end of the line, but not so anxious that I didn't think to empty the contents of the Super Sweeper onto the fire before dashing into the house. Safety First! So, I dumped and dashed. As vital as that phone call was to my 10-year-old self, I cannot recall who it was on the other end, for no sooner had I swept the phone to my ear, that a gust of wind blew a single burning leaf into the canvas catcher of our Super Deluxe Sears Leaf Sweeper. My Mother was screaming,
"Oh, my God, Jamie, get the hose!"
I dropped the phone. Our miracle lawn care product of the decade had become engulfed in flames and was burning to a crisp, right down to the charred aluminum ribs and nubs of those once shiny brown bristles. The smoke had dissipated, the alarmed neighbors had retreated, the metal was still hot and smoldering, standing testimony to the Super Deluxe disaster, when I heard the sound of Dad's '59 Chevy Impala's tires popping the driveway gravel; simultaneously snapping the fragile sinew of my own self-esteem. I promised to pay Dad back from the money I earned mowing lawns but I knew there would be nothing to cut until spring. On a positive note, it was a much sweeter fragrance than couch. The next week passed about as

slowly as had my first ten years.

MONDAY - 9/4/17

By Tuesday, Dad was admitting that it had been another unfortunate accident and if I hadn't been called into the phone and blah, blah, blah, I could have been hurt; music to my ears. By Wednesday at dinner, I was feeling empowered enough to mention that a new TV series was premiering the following night. It was to air at 8:30 and was called Zorro! All the kids at school had Zorro-itis, and I was starting to feel as if this was going to be a more than memorable Thursday, in a good way for a change. Change is inevitable but also often inconveniently time-sensitive. At dinner, I prepped the parents with talk of all of the commotion at school about Zorro as I deftly cut a deal. If I took my bath and was ready for bed in my P.J.'s, I could watch Zorro if I immediately went to bed at 9. Deal! I was in the tub by 7:30 and set about scrubbing and rinsing and scrubbing and rinsing, repeat. I wasn't dawdling; indeed, I was furiously setting about the business of clean. As the now grey water churned around my body, I heard a massive crash and the air pressure in the bathroom changed with an audible swoosh, bang, then a squeal. The squeal was my mother's voice letting out a squeal of shock, but it sounded like it had come from the open bathroom door,
then Dad shouted,
 "What the hell?!"
I looked at the door and was shocked to see it was still closed. As my gaze drifted down, I saw my whole family, standing, in the family room, looking up at me through the dripping, gaping hole that used to be our bathroom floor. I was in so much trouble I knew even Zorro wasn't going to save me. If there had been a tramp steamer docked in land-locked Youngstown, I would have hopped it. But I couldn't leave town as I still held the trump card, the secret. The time was fast approaching when there was to be full family disclosure and I couldn't miss that. As luck would have it, two months
passed without me generating any noticeable blackness. Every week Thursdays loomed on the calendar like a pendulum in the pit of my stomach

TUESDAY 9/5/17

I forgot to mention last night that the only other excitement, in the following month of Thursdays, was thanks to my Dad who climbed up on the roof of our garage with a .22 caliber rifle. No need for concern. He had to shoot a rat that had fallen into the deep end of our wintery waterless swimming pool. The rat apparently did not know how to use the ladder, his only option to escape certain death, so he took a slug right between his beady little rodent eyes as damn near the whole neighborhood gathered in our backyard to witness the violent and rather spectacular assassination. Understand that in the late fifties, a man perched on a roof with a rifle attracted an enthusiastic crowd. Thanks to Speck, Oswald, Ray and whoever that guy was on the grassy knoll, you can hardly get anyone to turn out for those types of events anymore, even if you give away free T-shirts. Fueled, I think, by the high-octane intensity and public adulation from the rat's demise, my father, the triggerman, pulled the family into the living room and made public the treasured secret that had become such a source of imagined power for me.

"Kids,"

He said, pausing just long enough to make you think that he was about to announce that he was going to become a sharpshooter for Orkin.

"Kids," he reiterated,

"Your mother and I told Jamie about this a few months ago, but now it's time for you

girls and your grandmother to know."

My sisters shot me a wary glance with a wary. A-ha, Grandma hadn't known after all.

-Your Mother and I are getting divorced...?

-Your Mother and I are Commie Spies...?

What was he going to say?

He said,

"I received a promotion at work."

Insert a collective sigh of relief!

"It's good news. I got a very substantial raise at work."

The big shoe was about to drop...

"It means we'll all have to move away for a few years."

The moment hung in the air...

" From each other?"

"No, sweetheart, all of us will move together, to England."

"Waaah," abruptly cut the stillness.

Grandma did a great Fred Sanford, as she clutched her heart and deftly popped her nitro! My sisters of 7 and 9, chimed in,

"Is that in Ohio?"

"No, it's across the ocean, kids. In the Old Country.

The girls sobbed, creating a Greek chorus of, "Waaah" in perfect four-part

harmony. Everyone cried except for my dad and me. He looked at me knowingly, and I looked back unknowingly but pretending that I, in fact, knew exactly what he thought I must have known what he was thinking. But, I couldn't tell if he was thinking...the Smoldering Couch, the Blazing Leaf Sweeper, the Gaping Bathroom Floor or the uncertain adventure ahead. I could see courage in his eyes, and I knew

I would have to rise to that bar he had just set with his gaze.

Six weeks after dad had broken the news to the family, we arrived in England, on the Queen Elizabeth I. Mom had insisted we see our country before traveling to another, so three weeks hence we had embarked upon a whirlwind tour of Washington D.C. and then to New York City where we saw *The Sound of Music* with Mary Martin (front row center for $10 a seat). One of my dearest friends, Phil Proctor, played Rolfe and I missed him by a few months. We ate Lychee Nuts in China Town and were squired around the city for two days by a cabbie named Al Schwartz. Dad had insisted that we go to England on a ship, just as he had come to America in 1926, on the Queen Mary, when he was only three. Then in 1943, he went to fight in Europe on the very same ship with thousands of troops. When Al Schwartz got us to the dock, Mom and Dad, Cindy, Linda and I got out of the cab and right there in front of us, was a blue wall of steel and rivets, the Queen Elizabeth I, towering above us, in all of its enormous Old-World grandeur. Al said his farewells and Dad graced him with a generous tip and as our bags were being cleared away we realized that Cindy was nowhere to be seen. Our largest bag, a steamer trunk, was taken away revealing Cindy lying flat on her back, on the pier. Apparently, when we all got out of Al's taxi, she had started looking up at the ship and never stopped until she fell over backwards in a dead faint. It was indeed, enormous. During the 5-day crossing Linda conveniently disappeared and Mom immediately jumped to the conclusion that she had fallen overboard, screaming,

"Turn this boat around, God Damn It." Mom, not Linda, had jumped prematurely, as Linda was soon found enjoying a sundae in the First-Class Dining Room. It was Cunard, in 1960, and there were three classes on the ship. We were in 2nd class. You could spot the passengers in third class by the shackle scars on their ankles and the lingering stench of gruel on their breath. One-day the ship's gyroscope ballast, which kept the ship level, gave out and Her Highness made a sharp U-turn. When she did, a very proper English woman, whose chair wasn't chained to the floor, went sliding in front of us sitting perfectly erect with teacup and saucer in hand. A film clip that will always replay in my memory. In 2nd class, they showed the same movie all week, three times a day. It was Elvis Presley and Tuesday Weld's *Wild in the Country.* I fell in love with Tuesday Weld for the rest of my life that week. She played a backwoods southern tramp in dirty bare feet with a willowy cotton print dress. I knew that I would have to wait at least three years before I could return to the States and marry her. She will love me like she loves Elvis. I will buy her shoes.

When we arrived in Southampton, a train took us to London, where we transferred to Saint Pancreas Station. Yes, we would pass through a train station named after an excretory organ, or moreover some saint of the lower digestive tract would be, a precursor of meals to come. But this was a new culture, and I lied to myself that I was ready to adapt. Arriving safely in our future hometown, sunny Bedford. We were surrounded by raining colorless, drizzling, bone splintering cold. It seemed as if the clouds from which the rain poured, were about 3 feet above our heads. It rained for 2 solid months as I recall. It was England, and that was merely the weather. In an effort to rise above the gloom we joked that if Sunny Days were Golden, we would deem the gray days Silver. I launched into an impression of a British Weatherman,

"Tomorrow will likely be partly cloudy with a possible chance of clouds and a rather

cloudy tomorrow when we can look forward to some quite sunless activity becoming
overcast with no bloody chance of warmth."

The best Bridge Hotel Moment was thanks to John the Headwaiter, that stodgy, cologne saturated, crimson-faced English guy, who had somehow schmoozed his way into a headwaiter position, well above his vocational scores. He thought that he ran an absolutely smashing 5-star hotel restaurant. Then, he met the Amedicans that occupied most of the entire third floor of his hotel. From the moment we met him, he regarded our family as he might have viewed a horde of marauding food critics. He regularly attempted to amuse us, always managing to say the wrong thing.

"Amedicans shoot off their mouths like they shoot off their miss-aisles."

He quipped, expecting a laugh. My mother had to be physically restrained. John fervently prepared Steak Diane, table-side, with such pomp and overcooking that pouring *Thunderbird* over a Wimpy Burger would have been a better culinary option. Throughout the course of our stay, John wore a variety of hats. Not really 'hats,' three different toupees to be precise, not all at once mind you, but yes, three toupees. We had names for them. Johnny Jr. was the one he wore most of the time. It was neat and perfectly coiffed, quite dapper actually. Then there was Harry, a rat's nest of somewhat disheveled horse-hair that he wore offering that he merely hadn't had time to get to the barber. G.I. John was the shortest and the most folically correct. It was the one he wore after he had finally 'made the time' to get to his phantom barber. I always encouraged the ruse,

"Glad you squeezed that haircut in John, you were looking jolly ragged there Johnny!."

He thanked me politely and met my stare with a not-so-subtle sneer,

"Indeed, Master James."

Look, he knew that I knew! He also knew that everybody else knew! And, of course, everybody knew that he knew that everybody else knew! We were all living a lie, and everybody knew it! But not everybody knew that the Amedicans had named them, Johnny Jr., Harry, and G.I. John. One night at dinner he added a tad too much flambé to the Steak Diane and Harry was instantly set ablaze, crackling with a cacophony of pops and sizzles. A nimble and quick-witted Turkish waiter, let's call him Volkan, launched his entire four-foot-ten frame into the air and covered John's burning locks

with a nearby serviette as John careened into the kitchen looking all the world like a Tibetan Monk who was having second thoughts. Quickly re-emerging from the kitchen, we immediately recognized G.I. John. Even at eleven years, I saw a golden opportunity; you could drive a truck through. I quickly carpe'd the tempore, "Wow, that was fast John. Does your barber have a chair in the kitchen?"

I buttoned it with,

"Hope you gave him a good tip!"

Mom inadvertently ran defense for me, as she passed tomato soup through her nose.

THURSDAY 9/7/17

I saw the majestic grill of a British racing green 1960 Jaguar Mark III moving directly towards me. Instinctively I leaped into the warm, sweet-smelling leather of this sumptuous British classic, I turned and next to me was my young father, and I was on a well-remembered business trip with him to Scotland.
I woke up.
While my nurses, Lori and Brie, fussed with my I.V. bags and morning shots to my stomach. I never thought I would have ever said that. Meanwhile I tried to recapture the whole dream but all that I could remember was the Jag and my first time in Scotland. I think that he must have taken me out of Bedford School for this trip because I remembered driving through the gates that day. Dad was born in Scotland in 1923. They lived in a "wee hoose" in Prestwick. His dad, Albert Edward Alcroft was a Golf Pro who had achieved much notoriety in 1920's Scotland. I learned that Grandpa and Dad and his brothers hadn't been the only athletes in the family. My grandfaither's faither was the National Swimming Champion of Scotland in the late 1800's and his son, my grandfaither's brother, was in his time, Scotland's National Champion as well. One day, they were having a stroll across Troon Golf Course, to the beach and a wee lad was crying by the quarry on the 16th hole because his sailboat was hung up in the reeds. Without hesitation, my grand-uncle waded into the dark quarry and as he began to make his way toward the toy boat, he got caught up in the reeds and pulled under. His Faither jumped in after him and they both drowned. I have the newspaper clipping from 1888. My grandfaither was born 3 months later and he never liked the water. It turns out, my Dad had been instructed by Mom to drive me to Scotland and tell me about the birds and the bees, that in 1960's England were birds in mini-skirts. He didn't, wouldn't, and ultimately never did. I've faked it my entire life. He still had family in Scotland and he dropped me off at the modest council house of Peggy Macpherson and Agnes Strathairn. My Aunt Peggy and Aunt Agnes were in their early 50's, though they seemed ancient to me. They had lived together since they were both in their early 20's and did so until Agnes' death at 87. Peggy passed at 94 in an Elderly Home in Ayr. When Peggy was a little girl her mother sent her off to school one morning and by supper, her mother was dead. It was the European Plague of 1917 that took so many, so fast! Her mother had been my grandfather's sister and Peggy's father was a drunk that had left them penniless years before. The plague spared him but he was nowhere to be found. So, Peggy went to live with my great-grandmother and was raised by her on the periphery of being an Alcroft and always feeling as if she was part of the family. Over the years she and my Dad's older brother, Andy, became very close for first cousins. They eventually fell in love, and one day they were caught walking hand in hand, on the beach by one of the church ladies. When my grandfaither took the job as golf pro in Youngstown, he was able to sponsor and get all of the Alcroft's over to the states by 1927. All of the Alcroft's except for Peggy. There happened to be a letter in her file from a prominent member of the church describing her '...unholy hand holding with her cousin on the beach' as 'An incestuous sin against the Holy Father.' With all the Alcroft's gone to America, Peggy moved in with her best friend, Della Strathairn. Later that year Della was killed by a run-away horse-drawn milk truck and at the funeral she met Della's younger sister, Agnes, whose

husband had just left her for a stool at the pub. Agne moved in with Peggy for the next 58 years. I listened to these stories, and so many more, after Dad dropped me off with my aunties whom I loved and had often visited over the years, I vividly remember nights by the fireplace listening, singing and laughing. The big treat was on those nights when the Fish & Chip Van would come down the street ringing its bell. They'd send me out, with three shillings, for three bags! Yum.

I visited them again in the early 90's when I was doing a British Chat Show for Thames

Television. Agnes had sadly become blind due to failure of optic nerves. We were getting ready to go out to tea on a Sunday afternoon and Peggy had left her purse upstairs in her room. She said,

"Jamie darlin', would you mind fetching my purse for me son?"

I sprinted up the stairs to her room, stopping short upon seeing an 8x10 photo of my Uncle Andy on her bed stand. The walk on the beach had been over for sixty years ago but holding his hand had never ended for Peggy. True love never dies, but Andy

did. He was killed in WWII at the Battle of the Bulge.

At our tea that afternoon I asked,

"Agnus, what's the worst part about being blind?

She didn't skip a beat and shot back,

"The worst part is that I canna see, ya' daft boy!"

Peggy chimed in,

"I'll tell the worst part of her being blind. She always wakes me up in the middle of the night, calling out from her room." 'Peggy, what time is it? Is it morning yet?'

"Auch aye, it drives me rund the bend."

We laughed, and I had a thought. Sony had just come out with a hand-held device, a

calculator and a clock that had a voice. It was a man's voice that told you calmly and

clearly the date and time, anything you prompted him to tell you. When I went to London, I bought it and sent it to Agnes. She sent me a lovely note thanking me for my thoughtfulness and said that she loved it, and used it every day. Several years later I went back for a visit. We laughed, as we always had, and Agnes reiterated how much she loved the voice clock that I had given her. Peggy stiffened and offered,

"Well, to tell the truth, Jamie, I cannie staund the thing."

I turned to look at her, as Agnes also turned toward Peggy's voice,

"I'll tell you the truth Jamie, it was bad enough when Agnes would call oot to me in the middle of the night. Now there's this man in her room who wakes me up at all hours of the night with, 'It's three twenty a.m.' Or, 'it's four forty-four a.m.' It's never ending.

I tell you the man never shuts up! It's just terrible."

There was an awkward moment, and I said,

"Well, I'll get you one too, Peggy."

She considered the offer and said,

"Ach, no Jamie, one man in the hoose is quite enough!"

We laughed so hard! We always laughed.

FRIDAY 9/8/17

It was Thatcher's day off as "Budtender" at The Timothy Leary Memorial Medical Marijuana Clinic and he decided to hang out with me for a bit. This was a major commitment from a 24-year-old on his day off! Very cool. We started reminiscing about all of the parent-teacher conferences his imaginative antics had inspired. I told him my favorite was the time he flummoxed his teacher when she asked if he knew what perseverance was. He said,

"Sure, perseverance is when Mom can't find her purse, but she keeps looking for it anyway!"

She asked what he had been working on and he explained that he was writing an essay on semi-precious gems. Thinking she was going to catch him up in a fib, she challenged,

"Thatcher, can you tell the class the names of some of these semi-precious gems?"

"Oh sure, my favorites are Hematite, Rhodochrosite, Malachite, Labradorite, Azurite,

oh and one more GESHUTITE!"

The class cracked up! He was on a roll, so, he hit them with the button,

"Oh, and there's one I always have with me."

She bit,

"Which one is that?

"Myappetite!"

I feel obliged to illuminate that I had a collection of semi-precious gems from my silversmith days, and we had poured over them for hours, so he knew the names. We would take out the stones and gaze at their zat together. Now, how many fathers do that? I'd like to know. Speaking of geshutite, that was the year Thatcher caught one of those awful spring flu/colds and we spent a week nursing him back to health. On the day he was feeling well enough to go back to school, we decided, much to his delight, to keep him at home "just one more day." I thought we could watch a classic old black and white together so we curled up on the couch with a box of Kleenex and a big bowl of popcorn and watched Cyrano De Bergerac, starring Jose Ferrer. Thatcher loved that someone had a nose more significant than mine and he really got into the story. Success! I was exposing my son to the classics!

A week into the summer break I was at one of his baseball games, he was pitching. A mother of one of his friends came up to me and said,

"I want to thank you for Thatcher and the way he got Devon and Laura together. They are so happy together, just look at them!"

What, they were in fourth grade and 'so happy together!?'

I quipped,

"Huh?"

She explained that without Thatcher and his flower business, Devon would never have been able to woe Laura. She elaborated that Thatcher had set up an off-campus, after-school business, where, for a mere $3.00 fee, he sold a bouquet of flowers, a poem and gave lessons on how to present the two. It had been quite successful. A-ha! I wondered why that for the last three weeks of school he had chosen to walk, rather than ride his bike. Now I knew it was so he could pick his inventory. He had found an off-campus location where he kept buckets of flowers and

wrote poems. When I asked him about his Flower Business, he said,
  "Oh-Oh."
He confessed that he had made $36.00 in three weeks.
  "That's more money than I make playing poker at lunch, Dad."
Poker at lunch?
  "And, look how many people I brought together."
My father had once told me Dad once told me,
  "If you don't have cash, you're an animal."
No son of mine was going to be an animal. I reprimanded him for picking the
neighbor's flowers. He knew, full well, that he was wrong. When I thought of him and

his antics, I could only anticipate what my future might hold, and I smiled. I guess this

must be joyful parenting. By the way, thank you, Edmond Rostand! Thatcher had a
much more raucous and free-form sense of humor than his sisters. He entertained
family, friends and strangers without really trying. None of us will ever forget the night

we were in a favorite Italian restaurant, where the wait people sang. Wait, actors who

are wait-people, singing, in Los Angeles? What are the chances? So, a waiter
launched into That's Amore, and proceeded to troubadour through the dining room,
timing the song, perfectly, so that just before he got to '…that's Amore', he stuck the
microphone into the face of an unsuspecting customer, usually with a fresh mouth full

of pasta. It got old, fast. As he made his way around the room, he headed for our
table, egad! He had just finished singing, 'When your love turns to goo like a pasta
fasul'. He put the microphone to my young son's eager face, as Thatcher cut loose
with his best Durante,
  '…that's annoying!'
The entire restaurant burst into laughter and deafening applause causing our
wandering troubadour to cut his troubing short for the night, as I now do.

SATURDAY 9/9/17

If I'm honest, Thatcher got his love for attention through laughter from me. I did stand up, for a living for 40 years and because his Mom is an Emmy Winning, Ice Skating World, Canadian and USFA Hall of famer he comes by it quite naturally. The allure of the stage began for me in first grade when I played Joseph in a living nativity scene. Fourth grade saw me in Black-Face as Nat King Cole singing, *It Was Just One of*

Those Things. Forgive us father for it was 1958. Conrad Birdie and Emile De Becque

in High School lead to Alfred P. Doolittle and, yes, The Tinman in College. I retired from "the boards" for at least five years and then my thespian renaissance began

when Ron Maranian, The Armenian Comedian, and I became great friends, brothers. He performed an epic percussive poem, written by Marc Spiegel, entitled Fo-Fo-the- Bo, short for Food for the Body. It was a 14-minute tome about a mythical King who, when attacked by marauding hordes, would cook a banquet style vegetarian feast for them and peace would prevail across the well-fed kingdom. Ron and I drove across country together a few times for his various gigs. He thought I was funny so he wanted

me on stage with him. I conspired to play percussion for Fo-Fo-the-Bo, not the drums

or even a tambourine. I played the Triscuit Box. I'd be invited out on stage, and I'd sit

on a stool with the Triscuit Box and a couple of drum brushes. Before we started, I'd "tune" the box by removing and eating a few of the crackers. It got a good laugh. One

night Ron was opening for Richie Havens in Gainesville, and the University auditorium was packed with at least 1200 students. Richie's plane was late, and the promoter kept going out to tell the clamoring fans that the show would start, very soon.

An hour later Richie's plane landed, but it was a 45-minute drive from the airport. The

promoter asked Ron how much 'time' he could do and Ron assured him,

"Well, I don't know…About 20 minutes, I guess…but I…" The promoter, not listening,

told Ron,

"Great, terrific…get ready. You go on in five."

By now the entire audience were chanting,

"Richie, Richie RICHIE!"

It was deafening. Ron turned to me and yelled,

"We'll open with Fo-Fo-the-Bo."

It might have been a question. Hiding behind Ron, I was frozen with fear as we approached the curtain split. An old black man was sitting at the curtain split, to open

it as he had done for hundreds of entertainers over time eternal. Ron and I stood there and shook off the nerves, not! The old man looked up at Ron with sad, drooping, yellowing, blood-shot eyes and, as the crowd started going crazy and stamping their feet, he proffered,

"I don't know who you is brother but I sure as hell hope you is RICHIE!"

SUNDAY 9/10/17

Well, they hauled my I.V. ass down to surgery today for another look at my old ticker. They must have started me on my twilight time before I left the room because I was happily woozy when we hit the elevator. We stopped at one floor, and I exclaimed,

"Third floor, lingerie, biopsies, random limbs, bagpipes and brain transplants."
My attending nurse offered,

"We can start the anesthesia early if you'd like Mr. Alcroft."
We left the elevator and crossed to another hospital tower that was an open-air bridge. We must have moved into the gurney-pool lane because the speed combined

with the warm Santa Ana winds swept me back to Key West as a rush of warm wind engulfed me in a familiar warmth. I was meandering through Key West on my trusty 10-speed Island Cruiser, remembering the Key West of 1976 there were few cars but

everyone had a bike. Babies were carried in quilt-lined front bike baskets, with another

baby on the back and maybe even one in the oven.
Somewhere on the island, great Vegetarian Feasts gathered every night and if you didn't know where it was, you could cruise up and down the frond-dappled streets with a salad or a Tofu Casserole in your bike basket, probably under your baby, until you came across scores of bikes parked in front of a Victorian gingerbread, 'Conch' house.

Converging at the southernmost tip of pure lust and purest love It was both the end of and the beginning of unbridled innocence. We were well fed with smiles and warm

hugs as we ate good food, smoked great weed, ate again, talked and laughed and told each other our lives. Then we'd smoke, or did I already say that? Laughing again,

and dancing to the fantastic mixes served up by Frisco Bob that he rolled out of a 500-watt AM radio station; WKWF, Wonderful Key West Florida. Bobby was an icon,

a magic-music making legend on The Rock. I usually left the feast just as everyone was getting naked. Silly me. I'd bike back to my jewelry store on Duval Street through

the warm, moist air and create; stoned and sated, listening to the radio long into the cool night - the best time to pound silver. Through the music and the soft roar of acetylene, texture and dimension leaped from the tip of my torch. I could see it all before me. The magic that was the island inspiring me in its warming embrace. Out of my hands yet deep within my heart.

MONDAY - 9/11/17

A few blocks from my jewelry store on Duval Street, WKWF was broadcasting from the top floor of the La Conca, the highest building in town, a four-story hotel right in the center of our low hanging island. It was an AOR format, which meant they could play anything they wanted, and they did. But there was a catch: The commercials were as terrible as the music was great. Over many nights of listening, somehow a latent marketing enzyme was released into my body. It could have been purely physiological, or just due to my damn Jupiter going retrograde. I don't know how I got
up the nerve to get in the elevator that day...but I knew as I rode up those four stories
to the station, I must be on a mission. I told myself that I was performing a public
service and I was about to tell *The Man*, something he needed to hear. Wait a minute;
I rode up on an elevator in Key West in 1976? It almost pushed my belly into my windpipe. I hadn't been in an elevator in years. Wow, I had to get off The Rock more often…but then, I was afraid I'd miss a feast. I took a deep breath hoping my innards might soon fall back into place and I asked to speak with whoever might be in charge
of commercial production. Out walked the program director, Tom Corcoran. (Who is now a respected mystery writer and at the time was Jimmy Buffet's sailboat Captain and closest confidant). I think I closed my eyes as I said,
   "I love your music. Everybody loves the music, we all love your music, really, it's
   incredible but the commercials are kinda' terrible and hard to sit through just waiting
for such great music, which we love, we really love, it's great. The music I mean; and
I do a lot of impressions and voices and if you need me to come in and do a few of them for your commercials, I'd be happy to do it ......for free." I had yet to breath.
Opening my eyes, I saw Tom, still standing there, smiling oddly.
   "This is great!"
He said, expecting him to follow with a hearty mocking yet sympathetic laugh. Tom continued,
   "This is my last day. I just quit. Frisco Bob is taking over my job, and we need a
   production manager and a 'Morning Man,' can you start tomorrow?"
I had yet to breath.
   "Ever run a board before?"
No answer. Hell, oxygen's overrated anyway.
   "That's okay I'll get our afternoon guy to come in early and show you. You'll go on the air at 6 am tomorrow…I'll get you keys to the station. You can come in around 5:30 and get comfortable." I must have breathed. Because for the next three years, I was there at 5:30 am every weekday morning picking out my show from the vast library of 33 1/3 vinyls. One morning I was locked out of the station, and I climbed three stories up a drainage-pipe and crawled through the bathroom window to get on
the air by six. Guess which Beatles song kicked off my show?

The 5 A.M. rides to the station engulfed by the soft cacophony of the rising day were always magical. I'd tack back and forth going the wrong way down one-way Olivia Street, smelling the sunrise between the gusts of the warm windy still fragrance of Frangipani. Think honeysuckle with a 'kick.' Olivia Street was infamous for the town cemetery, where the iconic epitaph, *I Told You I Was Sick!* still exists. Pedaling my way through the puddle-pocked back streets, I'd often find other islanders cycling home from a long night out. They would quite often shout out requests as we passed.

One muggy morning there was a girl on a bike, an old flame, riding toward me and without a word we circled our bikes. She'd just arrived that night from Montreal and finally said,

"Je t'ai cherché toute la nuit."

Well, she found me. We simply fell into each other's arms, our bicycles magically slipping away beneath us. We found ourselves at Louie's, deserted, backyard as that

deep low sky started to pour thick warm rain. Forgetting where we were, we became

lost in each other's longing, for as long as we dared. I'd been captured again by the magic of this French-Canadian beauty with sea green eyes.

I got to the station and went 'on the air' a little late that morning. No one on the island

noticed. My 'ratings' must have been through the roof, right? When I did go on

the air, I started speaking in mid-sentence as if the signal had been interrupted by

some spectacular inter-stellar anomaly, which, in part, was true. I played Jesse Colin Young's *Sunlight* and kept my job.

"*Like a tree in the meadow wind*
She will bend to take you in,
Makes no difference where you been
That's the way she feels about you...."

I can hear Jesse's vibrato now. Perfection-n-n-n. I'd get off the air at 10 am and launch into writing copy and recording some totally whacked out commercials. It didn't matter what I did because it was always better than what had come before. Sometimes I'd just put on a sound effects record and read the copy ad-libbing to the sounds the record threw my way. It was improv, totally random comedy unexpectedly careening over the path of my life. I'd grab a Cuban lunch swimming in Crystal Hot Sauce at El Cacique, head for the beach and then the jewelry bench. The Beach and the Bench.

The first hand-delivered note I received at the station was given to me at about 6:30 in morning by a small man in a big hat. How he got into the station, I'll never know. The note had been written in Matanzas, Cuba and was scribbled on the back of a grocery store receipt. It read: 'Listening at all nights to hear Freedom from r. heavens." Freedom from the rich heavens? Oh, they wanted to hear Richie

Haven's song Freedom. Wow. There were several amigos huddled around a

radio
somewhere in Cuba, clandestinely listening to a 'skip wave' from a 500-watt AM radio station in Key West? The note had been hand delivered not mailed. I passed it off to Frisco. Radio Free Cuba, muy bueno!

I was usually funny when I had an audience, hell, even an audient. This hospital gig hasn't been any different. One day, in Key West, my live-in sweetheart, D.D., told me that if I thought I was so fuckin' funny…I should prove it at the Ed Sullivan Show. If memory serves, we may have been having some sort of altercation at the time, you think? Ed Sullivan had been dead for ten years, but a guy named J.P. Bo had resurrected him --- J.P. Bo (as of 2016, the top-selling Honda salesman in California) through his magnetic personality, became the Flo Ziegfeld of Key West. (spell check only shows me, Seinfeld and Siegfried, how pop culture is that?) Bo brought a guy named Frank Spencer to the island and produced a show called, *Frank Spencer is Lenny Bruce*, he wasn't, and not a lot of people cared. Frank was very talented and stayed in town for a couple more productions. Then Bo had an epiphany. He tapped the talents of an undercover hippie, a short-haired, indigenous fruit-eating, tennis pro, who got more pussy than Felix the Cat, named Lloyd Mager, to play the role of Ed Sullivan; a stroke of genius. Lloyd was the most unlikely Ed Sullivan impersonator since Shamu but it worked. The premise being that Ed had not died but had escaped to a life of sun, hashish and windsurfing in Cayo Hueso. Bo produced an Ed Sullivan Show the first Sunday of every month at the Greene Street Theater at 8 pm, just like the show on TV. It was a place where everyone who thought they had talent could prove that they did or didn't. A guy named David played the clarinet while his dog sang. It was merely the dog's reaction to the pain inflicted by David's wildly askew armature. Many years later David was seen on the TV show, Cops, getting busted for selling cocaine on
Thomas Street. He never left show business. He put the clip from the show on his
acting reel.
Anyway, my girlfriend, De De West had challenged me to do the show, and I did. I did a bit about bringing the romance back into masturbation. Originally conceived by Kenny Kramer, yes, that 'Kramer.' Kenny gave it to me, so I included it in my 20-minute set at the Ed Sullivan Show. That and my other stuff killed, I was floored. Two years of radio and so many Sunday's of Sullivan Shows passed by far too quickly. Then, one day, in 1978 I got off the air and was handed another hand-delivered note. It read,
'You must be one of the funniest men on the island; I'm the other one. Let's get together. Mack Dryden, 1116 White Street, upstairs.
I finished up my commercial production work for the day and rode my bike over to the corner of White Street and Olivia. Mack was sitting on his upstairs porch and waved me up. Turns out he was the same Mack Dryden (how many could there be?) who illustrated the Key West Cartoon Calendar. Everybody I knew had one hanging in their kitchen. Mack had supported himself for a few years with the cartoon calendar, his drawings, and several articles for the local papers. He listened to me on the radio and had seen me at the Greene Street Theater. He figured if we put our heads together, we could craft a sketch show that would knock Key West audiences off of their kollective keesters. He talked out some ideas that he had for sketches, and it got my creative juices flowing. Throwing some ideas back at him, we were laughing and fleshing out a show. I told him

that I had a bit
of trouble with the idea of writing sketches from whole cloth; I wanted to do Improv,
but I'd do characters in the sketches, help him produce and direct and I'd do a hunk of stand-up in the show. We vowed to meet again soon, and start putting the show together. We did just that.

THURSDAY 9/14/17

One quirk I quickly learned about the Key West of 1978 was that everybody was on *Island Time*. Many times, many people promised to pull forces and get together to create fantastic things that might change the world. They rarely did. It was manana land. If someone told you they would meet you somewhere at 2 pm, they might get there at 3:15 pm, find you waiting, and act as if nothing was amiss. The truth was, *Island Time* drove me crazy and I was about to learn that I wasn't the only laid forward person on this laid-back isle. Just like his note had said, he was the other one. The next day Mack left three or four typed-out scripts on my front porch. I read them and immediately went to White Street. I told him that we should talk to our cronies at the Greene Street Theater and secure a weekend in March. We had three weeks to cast, rehearse and mount the show. Mack came up with the name, *Vital Signs*. We put together the sketches, assigned the roles and essentially said, "Hey, everybody, let's put on a show!" Just like Mickey Rooney did with Judy Garland. Lately, I would see Mickey sitting in front of our grocery store in Westlake Village. He would sit there until he got recognized and then go home. Heather Locklear did the same thing at Starbuck's.

So, we opened on a Friday night to a sold-out crowd and closed on Saturday to a SRO house that all sprang to their feet at the last sketch and screamed for more. In the middle of our celebration that night, Mack told me that he thought he was going to start writing another show immediately. I joked,

   "Okay, just let me finish my drink."

He said,

   "I want to do the next one by myself."

He must not have thought my contribution to the success of the show was significant enough to partner up again. I was hurt and a tad furious, in that order. We didn't talk to or see each other for a couple of months, not an easy thing to do

on an island 2x3 miles, populated by people who came up to you every day and raved about how great OUR show had been. Mack's new show was called *Revenge of Vital Signs*. It opened on a Friday night in May to a sold-out and giddily

expectant house but the show closed the next night to a light crowd. Mack left the island with his girlfriend. They went to Maine in search of a mind-rinse and probably

lobster. My girlfriend, on the other hand, went away that summer to be a stunt woman in a Peter Benchley pirate movie, *The Island*, that shot in the

Caymans.

FRIDAY 9/15/17

Watching and waiting for that anonymous donor to pass. I'm aware of how morbid it is of me to even think like that but I'm getting a little, scratch that, a LOT fuckin'
batshit stir-crazy in this room as evidenced by my new hobby; getting snippy with my nurses. Gotta' watch that. No wonder I'm escaping to my halcyon days in the Keys.
The summer Mack was in Maine, I stayed at the station, worked the stage at the Pier House on the weekends, and watched the stunningly beautiful bartendess, Cindy G. pour drinks and laugh at me, until we fell in lust. Though I soon found out
that hanging with the goddess of late night meant never sleeping until dawn, I was
game, but just for a while. I liked daytime too much.
Mack returned to the island in late August and came by the station. He said that he wanted to do another show, together. I didn't blink and said,
   "Sure, but this time let's do it right!"
He didn't blink,
   "How do you mean?"
   "Well, let's give ourselves a chance to run for a few weeks. Let's pitch it to the
   Waterfront Theater, they've got 300 seats"
Mack was game, and I think he appreciated my not mentioning his *Revenge* from last May. We scheduled a meeting with the Board of Directors of the Waterfront through the radio station either sub-or-consciously distancing ourselves from the renegade Greene Street Theater. The Waterfront did Sondheim, Wilde, and Ibsen. The Greene Street did Albe, Ferlinghetti, and a decadent production of *Cabaret* replete with drag queens as Kit Kat girls. The Waterfront was supported by benefactors and Old Key West Money. Greene Street was supported by New Key
West Money. We never asked, Anyway, Mack and I got dressed in collared shirts, long pants, maybe even socks. I forget our exact level of sucking up. We presented our case to the board. We had the most talked-about, well-attended show in recent island history and we wanted to do another incarnation of our new, as yet unwritten, show in the most wonderful theater on the island in three weeks with an eye toward an extended run. They smiled cordially and explained that they currently had *The Importance of Being Earnest* running at the theater for the next two months. Impossible. We said that that would be no problem because our show was going to be a Midnight show every Friday and Saturday night. Impossible. We promised to use and never disturb their scenic design or lighting grid. We promised to work within their parameters, and leave the theater just as we had found it. Impossible. There was indeed, hesitation on their part. I chimed in that if we didn't sell out on the first night we would close the show....and give them 100% of the door, times two. Possible-just not pretty. They said, "Okay."
Mack set up a rehearsal hall at the local Baptist Church Hall and sent out a casting
call across the island. It was billed as an SNL-type Key West Comedy Review

78

and

people turned out in droves. We hadn't begun to flesh out the show, but we knew if we put together the right troupe of character actors, we could make the show work with and around their talents. Great talents like Tony Gregory, D. D. West, Sam Weyman, Joe DeLuca, Perry Halevy, even a guy named Bato who never showed up to rehearsal. The only exception was a girl from the Bronx, Darina Byrne, who was so wacky and hilariously undisciplined at the auditions, we had to

cast her! We started rehearsals the next day, taping the floor at the church with the rectangular dimensions of the Waterfront's stage. The rehearsals were scheduled for 1 pm every day and much to our surprise everyone arrived by 1:45 or 2 --- pretty

good for Key West. About three days into rehearsals, I was fired from the radio station. I was told it was because I had falsified time cards. It was really because my hero, Frisco Bob had a girlfriend who needed my job so they could afford to move to Madison, Wisconsin where Bobby had secretly accepted a new job at K-MAD. Ah, the convolutions of the airwaves! I found out the dirty truth after I had taken the station to court. What the hell, I sneaked into the station's offices one night, as I still had the keys, and stole files proving I had not falsified any time cards. I won a $2000.00 settlement, big money for 1978. The 2K would be worth $7,775.59 today. Yes, I looked it up!

It was May 23, 1979, Opening Night of the appropriately named *Son of Vital Signs*. As luck would have it, on that particular night, there was a hurricane coursing through the Florida Straits and the island was under mandatory evacuation orders from the Governor. We were determined to take the chance. We polled the cast and they were 'in' for taking the chance with us, too late for any of us to turn back and that 100% of the door, times two was looming large. By 11:30 that night there were over a hundred bicycles parked in front of the staid and proper Waterfront and the house was full, buzzing with 'buzzed' people. As the house lights went down, a spotlight hit stage right of the luxurious maroon velvet curtain, Darina strutted out, dressed in a sequined cigarette-girl costume. She held a large white card inscribed with the name of the first bit: The Fishing Sketch. She was met with a burst of thunderous applause. The jolt of pure sound shocked her, and she jumped in a startled skip step, pumping the volume even higher. She started across the stage, with a Carol Channing smile, kick- stepping along the taped line, she had been rehearsing on for weeks. About five feet from stage left, she stepped high and plummeted head first into the darkness of the orchestra pit! We had rehearsed with a taped-off rectangular stage plan. Alas, The Waterfront stage was curved. Rowena was down for the count, but as she had taken plenty of Quaaludes before the show, to quell her nerves, she wasn't hurt! We had our first, huge laugh and the curtain hadn't even opened yet! The growing hurricane force winds and rain intently pounding on the tin-roofed theater was barely audible over the cacophonous laughter that continued through this first performance. Backstage was craziness, total chaos. On stage, a lazy househusband with cardiac arrest was revived by a Marx Brother's style paramedic armed with a battery and jumper cables. Huge laughs! An undercover homeless guy, Bato busted a drug- smuggling street cop as the cop was hassling him for not wearing a shirt in public, Mack 'came out' as Stacie Sims, the flamboyant spokesman for the Save the Sissies Society that he delivered with a sibilance of typhoon force. Then, I nailed the irritatingly familiar back- up beeping of the Key West garbage trucks made on their pre-dawn raids! Where there had been three hundred audience members now there was a mass of people sobbing and heaving with laughter. Then we finished them off with a look at the weather from Mack's brilliant Helio Coptor. The hour and a half had flown by and our standing ovation went on for so long we eventually had to walk off the stage into the audience and escort the masses, still convulsing and twitching from *The Son* to their rain soaked cycles. The Hurricane missed the island that night but we blew them away. The show ran for three weeks. It was months later that Mack and
I received the Louis Carbonell Award from the Southern Florida Newspaper Writers Association for Best New Act of 1979. Maybe we were on to something?

SUNDAY 9/17/17

After the show closed, before Mack could tell me he didn't need me for the next one, I decided to pursue an idea I'd been kicking around for a while. Empowered by the success of the Waterfront show, I went over to the Casa Marina, a beautiful old Biltmore resort from the 1920's. Marriott had spent millions on its renovation, and it had become an upscale 'hot spot' on the rock. It took me a while to get to the right person after having to get past typical front desk personnel who would have been better suited asking me if I 'wanted fries with that?'. I introduced myself to 'the entertainment guy,' he recognized my name. I was in. I asked him why Sunday nights were dark in their beautiful Casa Marina lounge? He said that they couldn't get a crowd in that room on a Sunday night if they gave drinks away. I pitched him my idea, telling him,
  "I could fill it."
He asked,
  "What kind of budget would you need?"
$500, $600 and $750 flashed through my mind, but I said,
  "$1,500; pay me half the first three weeks and if I can put at least 100 people in the room pay me the balance of..."
I hesitated to do the math.
  "...the remaining $2,250 if I deliver."
He hesitated, I think he was doing the math too, and finally said,
  "Sure, let's give it a try."
I'd never made 'a deal' like that, ever, in my life but I knew this could be a great idea.
Key West has a nightly ritual called Sunset. Every place in the world had a sunset, but the one in Key West was a tribal ritual, populated in the older days by the native Conchs, named after the plentiful and slow-moving mollusk that had sustained them when they first came to those islands in the late 1800's. When hippies arrived in the late 1900's they started bringing baked goods, like Banana Bread and trinkets to sell and trade. In time, street performers started working the gathering crowds of tourists for hat money and there were some very professional and seasoned entertainers supporting themselves, in a rather meager, gypsy-like fashion. When I went to the Casa Marina and made my palm-sweating, seat-of-the-pants-deal, I was armed with the knowledge that the jugglers, tight-rope walkers, singers, fire-eaters, acrobats and magicians who worked the crowds for cash were lucky if they pocketed $50 to $75 before that burning orb of light gulped into the tranquil Gulf, closing their curtain for the night. I went to my favorite band in town Hearts of Palm, great guys, Woody, Din, Ron, and Quint. I affectionately referred to them as Parts of Ham. They agreed to be the house band for $75 each. Okay, I had $1200 left. I decided it would be fair to pay Mack $400 to write and be in comedy sketches ala Vital Signs, including a weekly news report. I took $500 for my hosting and producing and hired three street performers at $100 bucks each with the understanding that the street performers would do two sets. It was one hell of a good show. The band played me on, and I did some stand-up then I tossed it to the band that had an opening number. I came out and introduced *The Loco-Motion Circus*, a high-powered acrobatic street trio. They were played off by the band and we segued to a Mack & Jamie comedy sketch and so on, until the end of the first act. We took an intermission, so the bar

81

could make some money and then we continued to delight with the second act.

That first week, I had hung posters outside of every bar in town and spread the word with all of the hard-drinking sailors and shrimpers on the island. By the end of the first
three weeks, I had tapped out all of my unemployment settlement and was relieved to hear that Bubba, from the Casa Marina, thought it was working, so he paid me the
balance and I was flush and Dim Sum. Key West has Key Limes which are much smaller than regular limes. Key West has Key Deer which are much smaller than regular deer. Everyone on the island works for Key Wages, so this was to be a welcome boon to the economy. Though Key West now enjoys a bustling tourism industry year-round, in those days October and November were dead months. Tourist season didn't pick up again until after Christmas. The joke was, 'Why do they call it
tourist season if you can't shoot them?' We were still packing them in on Sunday nights but the patrons had shifted to the crowd from the Greene Street Theater and hippie fans of the street performers. I could only surmise that the Tourists had, in fact, been shot. The sailors and shrimpers had defected to Mike's Clam up the keys. The bar business fell off almost entirely as our new clientele could barely afford the $5 cover charge and came to the shows pre-ripped to the tits! I would overhear a giggling audience member say...
"Uhh, Um...", smacking his dry mouth, "six waters please, no ice."
I knew we were doomed, and sure enough, after the eighth week, Bubba bemoaned,
"We're barely breaking even, so look..."
"Thanks, Bubba, it's been great." I cut him off mid firing.

I haven't written about the smells of Cedars. Sometimes the strikingly bright punch of the alcohol pads manages to cut the stale sterile stagnancy of the hallways. Then they roll out the food carts to spice it up a little. I so wished I could still smell the sesame/honey/oats and turmeric fragrances that filled Key West's local health food store, The Herb Garden, owned by a renowned cocksman, named Richard, who was

right out of an R. Crumb strip. There was a 'spiritual being", and sexy little blond, not necessarily in that order, who worked there, named Maya. Though she was pure of body and mind and seemed at times to be almost levitating, she flirted like a Fort Lauderdale cocktail waitress and I flirted back like a conventioneer in Atlantic City. I always left the Garden with a bag of trail mix and a woody on the side. So, when I was ousted from the Casa Marina that day, I was in dire need of a carrot juice and maybe something on the side with my trail-mix. When I walked in, there was a guy at

the juice bar, so I ordered and he proceeded to juice my carrots with the same slow pace and the intensity with which a nuclear physicist might handle plutonium 238.
"Here man."
He said, as he set it, ever so gingerly, on the counter. I thought it might explode if I picked it up too quickly, so I just stared at it for a minute as the guy stared at me, as if
he was looking at a long-dead relative.
"I know you," He confessed.
"Sure…Past life, right? Nice to see you again."
He didn't laugh.
"No, you're the guy who put that scorpion in the capsule and beamed it out of the universe."
"Are you tripping?"
"Maybe a little still…don't know…probably, maybe a little. Did I, um, already say that?"
I sipped the juice slowly, reflecting on our scintillating conversation thus far.
I actually had covered an enormous scorpion with a Mason jar one night at a party as
it suddenly appeared in the middle of the living room carpet causing all to fall into complete silence. I wiped my orange mustache,
"Oh yeah, at Martha's house?"
"Oh, right, I was tripping that night, but that was really cool. You're Maya's friend, right?"
"Right," I said, looking around for her. "Where is she?"
"In Fort Lauderdale"
"When is she coming back?'
"She moved there a couple of weeks ago."
"Bummer," I said, as I thought to myself 'Bummer.'
He just stood there shaking his head as if he agreed with something very profound and holy. I finished my carrot juice, paid him and started to leave, resigned to the fact
that I wasn't going to get my 'usual.'

"Oh. Wait, you're the funny guy right?" he called out.

"One of them," I called back as I reached the door.

"Well she left this note for you," he smiled holding out a small letter. This guy really liked leaving things until the last possible moment. Walking back, I took the note,

"Thank you"

"No, thank you!" he protested.

"Uh?"

"For beaming up that scorpion. It's in a better place, fer sure."

"Riiiight. We all are."

I read the note as I was standing at my bicycle by the curb. Maya had left Key West to live with her single Mom in Fort Lauderdale. She had taken a job as, of all things, a cocktail waitress, at a club, called the Comic Strip. In the note, she wrote that Mack

and I were funnier than a lot of the comedians from the New York club who were performing there…for actual money. I went home and called the number at her Mom's

house, Maya answered. After we flirted, she explained, that The Comic Strip was a franchise of The Comic Strip in New York City. They bring four New York acts down every two weeks, put them up at a house close by and give them a car to drive. I asked if she thought we could get on stage and she said we had to audition on a Thursday night. She went on to say that there were some pretty funny people there right now. Some guys I'd never heard of…Paul Reiser, Rich Hall, Dennis Wolfberg and Jerry Seinfarb. She insisted that Mack and I would kill! Thanking her profusely, I told her that we'd see her soon. I immediately went to call Mack, but I knew he probably wouldn't answer. He never did, damn it! He didn't have a phone. So, I rode over to White Street and told him about the call. Color me surprised, he balked.

"We don't have an act. We can't compete with those professionals from New York. We don't have an act. What would we do? I can't, and I won't, we don't have an act! You can if you want to, fuck this!"

"Okay, I agree, you are absolutely right," I lied.

A couple of days later I ran into a guy I knew who co-owned Sloppy Joe's and a strip

club up the Keys, The Knotty Clam or something like that. He suggested that they might need some comedy up there. I gave him my phone number and the next day I got a call from him offering me $50 to do a 15-minute set between the acts. It was an

hour's drive and my 1950 Lincoln's starter had died out. This was 20 years before the

internet and an impossible part to find for this 28-year-old classic at the Southernmost

Tip, so I had no wheels. Wait, Mack had a car! He said that he'd drive me to the club

if I paid for the gas. I told him I'd buy him dinner and drinks. On the way up to the club

in Marathon, I pitched the idea of The Comic Strip again. He said,

"No! Flat out. No!".

He didn't yell, he was just very adamant, very adamant. I vowed to myself to convince him but I let it go for now.

We got to Mike's Clam Shack and went in. The door was right by the stage and there was a gorgeous girl with a wad of cash between her lips, no, not her mouth. Each of her ample breasts were in the mouths of two appreciative pirates, yes, actual

bald and tattooed pirates! The manager said,

"You're the comic? Oh, Jesus, where are you from?"

"Key West"

"Christ on a biscuit, seriously?" He tried to assure me.

Mack and I stood there fearing for our lives as we heard the off-stage announcer say,

"And now, Gentlemen, (notice, no Ladies) a very special treat."

They hooted and hollered with lecherous glee. He continued,

"A comedian all the way from Key West, he says he's funny, please welcome, Jeremy Albright!"

He gave it all he had, but it wasn't enough. They didn't welcome me. They berated me, they heckled me; they jeered their pirated jeers. Twenty bald-headed, tattooed drunks' fresh off the Pequod yelled seafaring obscenities at me but somehow, I actually prevailed and got some terrific laughs. More importantly, I got the audience's

attention, even though I had no tits and no…lips. The Guy gave me my fifty bucks. I don't even remember leaving the club. All I remember is riding back to The Rock in silence with Mack driving. After about 20 minutes he said,

"Okay…"

Lost in reliving those 20 minutes on stage, I asked,

"Okay! What?"

Mack mumbled, "…I'll do it."

Snapping out of my trance,

"Do what?"

"I'll do The Comic Strip."

I looked at him and his eyes didn't leave the road.

"If you can survive what you survived tonight, you can get us through anything."

All I could say was,

"Let's eat."

We went to the Full Moon Saloon, owned by Sid Snellgrove and haunted by Hunter S. Thompson, B. J. Martin, Lean Gene the Dancing Machine, Woman, Chicken, Tom McGuane, my buddy Glenn and the best fish sandwich ever made anywhere in the

entire world. Over sandwiches, I suggested that we drive up to Fort Lauderdale in three days for the 'Open Mike Night' and amazingly Mack agreed.

It was Sarah's birthday today. She turned 63 and she doesn't look a day over 35 and

a half. I swear, I am aging for two!

It was a five-hour drive to Fort Lauderdale, and we did it on a Thursday. A pugnacious little bastard named Joe Mullins met us at the door of the club and graciously offered,

"Take a fuckin' Number."

We did. Number 7, I felt lucky. Joe said,

"You guys together?"

I said,

"I don't know about him, but I haven't been together for years."

Mullins gave me that, don't try to be funny with me look, save it for the stage! The show started that night at 8 pm. I have no recollection of what we did to pass those four hours, I think we rehearsed in the car. When the show began there was total electricity in the air…it was magical…Mack and I knew exactly what we were going to do…we had a killer four minutes. That's all they allowed us…four minutes to prove what we could do…we were going to kill 'em. The act before us did an impression of the Bee Gees. Wait a minute, we do the Bee Gees, that's all right, we could regroup. I turned to Mack. He looked at me and said,

"I can't do this"

"What!"

"I can't do this; he just did the Bee Gees. We do the Bee Gees!"

Jeez, I thought I could get us through anything? I knew Mack well enough to know that we could do this…but he wouldn't, not that night. I turned to the Emcee,

"Just introduce Jamie Alcroft."

"What? Jamie who?"

"Jamie…Jamie Albright"

I left Mack standing there. He must have been petrified. I went up and did four minutes, got some laughs and got off. The cocky doorman, Joe Mullins, waited until the show was over and told me that I could come back anytime I wanted and I would

get 25 fuckin' bucks a set. We left the club at 11 pm and drove the five hours home in silence. I remember sitting on my front porch that morning, wondering what I was going to do as I watched the sunrise, already hot off the horizon. Paradoxically nothing

dawned on me.

Mack decided for us the next day by leaving some scripts on my front porch. The next week we drove up to the Comic Strip again and went on together. We killed, simply killed and Joe said WE could come back whenever we wanted, and we did. For the next four months, we drove the five hours to the club every Thursday and did five shows returning on Sundays to the rock. We slept in the club at night on the long benches and woke up every morning to the sound of the cleaning crew.We spent our weekdays back in Key West writing stuff to try at the club and as we learned the Fort Lauderdale comedy culture, and we started entering local talent shows on the weekends. Often, we would win $500. and split the $100. from the two show nights at the *Comic Strip*. One night we lost to a 'clogger' at a talent show and almost quit the business. It wasn't so much the money, okay, it was, but it was also the rush of working with the New York Comics. The same people I mentioned before, oh, his name was Seinfeld, not Seinfarb. Maya ended up falling for Mack, big time and he got to stay at her Mom's house. No cleaning crew within miles! No problem, I had my hands full of tail mix, from the club. It was still 1979. We were working there with Larry Miller, Jackie Martling, Rick Overton, Mark Shiff, Eddie Murphy, and Rich Shydner. They were all working out their material and so were we. We were workin' the big time, Fort Lauderdale! One night after our show in Ft. Lauderdale, a guy came up to us in the bar and asked if we would consider coming up to his club in St. Petersburg to perform. He said he would pay us $1000 for Friday and Saturday and put us up in a condo. Wow.The club was called *Mother Tucker's*. It was right out of the Bad Boy's Island in Pinocchio. A typical Florida den of iniquity, sexy waitresses, coke, Quaaludes, aswimming pool in the middle of the bar and of course backgammon! No donkey ears in sight, yet!

The owner was thrilled to see us and showed us the way to the condo. I think we might have been the first entertainers to stay there. He told us there would be two shows, at 9 and 11. I asked him if the crowd in the second show was much different from the crowd in the first.

"Hell no," he flatly replied.

"It's the same crowd."

Mack and I cracked our best smiles and waved as he drove merrily away. When he was out of sight, we did a slow burn turn to each other. I don't know who was more frightened or dumbstruck. We had 30 killer minutes of stage time; we needed another

30. We had about five hours to find it. I was dispatched to the local Publix market to grab chips, soda, and sandwich supplies while Mack set up his typewriter and a comedy command post at the kitchen table for our long day's journey into the first show at 8. We spent the afternoon hacking and slashing through every bit of material

we'd ever imagined doing and hobbled together another 30 minutes. We made it to the club with time to spare. It was a zoo...mobbed. The DJ had to yell over the crowd

to kind of', sorta', but not really, get their attention. Hitting the stage, we launched into

our Prince parody, something new, written in desperation that afternoon (The law of Comedy dictates that you start with something new so you can always recover with a sure-fire piece). 'Prince" killed and the night was ours! Both shows. The band we were opening for was called *Tampa*. They were excellent and kept the crowd going with those 70's sounds. Mack and I were held over at *Mother Tucker's* for two weeks.

Years later, while raising three kids in Westlake Village, California one of our neighbors told me that a friend of hers had a recording studio in town and she thought that he and I would get along. His name is Steven Jay, and I visited his studio. He gave me some 'wild tracks' to play around with on a Comedy CD I was producing. He was making a living, playing bass for Weird Al Yankovic's tours and as we talked, he mentioned that he had started in St. Petersburg with a band called *Tampa*. The next time we met, I showed him the newspaper clipping from the Tampa Bay/St. Pete

Times with both of our pictures in the ad. No accidents.

The night we rolled into NYC, driving Mack's olive-green 1970 Plymouth satellite, that had lovingly come to be known as *Ollie*, we had no place to stay and no prospect of work whatsoever. The comics at the Fort Lauderdale *Comic Strip* who had repeatedly told us we would be a smash in the City were going to be surprised to see us, maybe not as ecstatic as we were to be in New York City, but definitely surprised. We made our way through the Lincoln Tunnel and found *The Comic Strip* with the aid of something called "The Yellow Pages." In those days there were kiosks called phone booths on just about every corner and in each one you could find the tattered remains of a partial phone book. *The Comic Strip* was on 3rd Ave, between 70th and 71st. We found a parking spot about five blocks away, in front of a club called *Catch A Rising Star.* As we rounded the corner of 3rd Avenue, we saw the familiar Comic Strip logo and suddenly this particular night's air became oddly thicker with the anticipation that had just chosen to lodge in my lower intestine. Yet, something sparkled. There were a few customers milling around the outside bar and as we got close enough to see inside. We thought we saw a couple of faces that we recognized from the Florida club.

Mack grabbed me,

"Quick. Who's that? "As he urgently fell back on my unfailing memory.

"It's Ron Richards, and the guy standing next to him is Rich Hall. Rick Overton just went into the showroom."

Mack sighed,

"Oh…Right. Ron, Rich and Rick, right."

We walked up to the bar and noticed a doorman standing behind a podium, of sorts, admitting people into the showroom, the inner sanctum. We said hello to Ron and Rich and were amazed at how friendly they were.

"So, you made it to New York! Good to see you!"

Another voice chimed in; it was Carol Liefer,

"Hey guys, Jack and Mamie, right? So, you got a gig up here?"

"No," one of us admitted.

"Where ya' staying?"

"We dunno-"

"They're staying with me if they got a car."

We turned toward the voice, and it was Ron Richards.

"Yeah, Rich just moved out yesterday, so I've got some extra room if you guys don't

mind living in New Jersey."

I jumped on it,

"Sure, why not? I graduated from High School there."

"Oh, you graduated from High School?"

Jimmy Brogan chimed, "Another one of those Smart Comics!"

"Yeah, sounds great,"

Great, we had a place to stay, wow. Overton walked out of the showroom fresh off his set, sweating, wiping his face with his hand. Noticing us, he lit up,

"Hey Guys, The Mackandjamia Nuts! So, you're in the Big Apple huh?"

"Yep."

"Where're you staying? "

"With Ron in New Jersey."

"Cool, you going up tonight?"

"We dunno, don't think so."

Rick turned to the guy at the podium.

"Hey, Lucien, these are those funny guys I was telling you about from Florida."

Lucien looked us up and down.

"You the guys from Florida?"

Mack started, "Well I'm from Mississ ---"

I cut him off, confirming, "Yeah, we're the guys...from Florida."

"Okaay-y-y-y right...I heard about you...from Joe.

"Who, FUCKIN' Joe?" I broke the ice.

"Ha, yeah, FUCKIN' Joe," he smiled.

"Tell you what guys. Gilbert dropped out, and...."

Looking at his roster,

"He was going up next. You want the spot?"

I chimed in,

"Sure."

I didn't dare look at Mack and share his terror. But I did and off of my steely glare with

abject fear in his voice, he bravely quivered,

"Sure. Ah, but, um, we'll need two mikes. "

Lucien suddenly was flummoxed, nay, irritated, "Two mikes, really?"

I backed Mack up.

"Yeah. We can't share a mike. Mack's had a recent outbreak."

"Okaaaay-y-y then," Lucien said. "Jerry's up now, you can follow him."

Jesus, Mary, and Joseph Cotton! We hadn't been in New York for an hour, and we had a place to stay and were about to take the stage at the Comic Strip following some guy named "Jerry." They were still trying to hook up that second mike while the

consummate pro, Hiram Kasten was introducing us. All the comics were sitting in a big semi-circle booth at the back of the showroom and more comics piled in to see how we'd do. We killed. Just did ten minutes and it was magic...over too soon. In the

afterglow, we followed a couple of the comics over to *Catch*, near where our car was parked. Ron Richards was with us, and he grumbled all the way over about how much

he hated Catch and the "downstairs" scene. We walked in, not-so-greeted by, heads

turning, and I could tell in an instant it was a much more high-stakes "Industry" scene

than the Strip had been. I could feel the vibe of money, power, and powder.

Comedy in America was about to get glamorous. This is where it would begin it's slow crawl from the primordial slime of smoky jazz clubs onto the land. A guy named David Saye was MC'ing that night, and the policy was that the MC put the show together. He set the line-up of comics for the evening. After we'd been there

for a few minutes, Ron Richards walked over to talk to him. I didn't recognize anybody in the outer bar, definitely a different group of comics than The Strip. I

saw David look over at us and shake his head, no. The evening had been too good
to be true, we couldn't have hoped for more, but we apparently weren't getting it; more, that is. Rieser, Maher, and Seinfeld walked in a few minutes later, and I could see by Saye's greeting that they were going on. Maybe it wasn't such a different crowd after all. I had to pee, and one had to walk through the showroom to get to the bathrooms. The room was only about 25 feet deep, but it was 75 feet
long. The stage in the middle of the room faced a 75-foot wall mirror. As I was making my way across the back of that interminable room, there was a comic on

stage named Richard Belzer. Reptilian in appearance, he backed it up with a split tongue-lashing assault on the audience and even the empty chairs around them. He had just sung, to the tune of *Stormy Weather*, "Don't know why---there are cum
stains on my tie, sloppy blow job." Well, I guess that "set the tone" for the room. He got a huge laugh, and as it was dying down, he called out to me walking across
the back to the Men's Room.
"Hey Sparky! What's the deal? You know, real men could hold their urine?"
Big laugh, he was on a roll. My surprise and sudden fear, froze me in his hollow eyes.
"Here's a specimen cup," he said as he reached down to a table in front and grabbed an empty wine glass. He tossed it to me. I was only about ten feet away from him, so I caught it and kept moving through this instantly pixilated, slow-motion world and glided into the Men's Room. What was I going to do? I was as good as on stage at *Catch* and Mack wasn't anywhere to be seen! The bathroom was really small, and as I stood at the urinal, I heard two guys, I guessed, in the stall, either snorting coke or maybe "just smelling it." I finished up and still had no idea how long I'd have to stay in there until this Belzer guy got off the stage. I started sweating when the coked- up guys stumbled out of the stall. One of them had a glass of Chablis in his hand, and I saw my way out. I offered him $20 for that
glass of wine and he took the deal. They left, and I could still hear Belzer berating the audience. I poured the wine into the glass Richard had thrown at me, and walked out of the Men's room heading directly for the stage. He saw me coming with glass in hand, half full of yellow liquid.
"Oh shit," he laughed into the mike.
I handed him the glass and whispered, off mike,
"It's Chablis."
He took it, and the audience laughed as I made a hasty retreat back to the bar, looking all the world like a civilian. I looked over my shoulder just as he smelled the liquid and recoiled. Milking at least a minute of laughs out of merely holding the
glass in his hand, he must have chugged it, because the roar from the crowd turned
every head in the outer bar. Overton said,
"What's Belzer doing; my act?"

90

'He's killin' 'em,' was the bar buzz. As Saye disappeared into the showroom, he signaled to Jerry that he should get ready. Belzer said goodnight to a thunderous ovation. When he walked out of the showroom, he was instantly surrounded by his

people, Buddy Morra, Rich Fields, and Rick Newman. Belz, as I was soon to know

him, started to walk out of the club with these luminaries and bevy of 'hopefuls' clamoring about him. On his arm was a beautiful blond and as he passed me at the bar he looked over and said,

"Good laugh Sparky, funny, thanks."

That's all I got that night, but weeks later I would learn that despite Belzer's acid tongue and cool 'tude' on stage, he was one of the warmest guys I would ever know. He was, after all, "The Belz".

It was two years later we did our first, of two, Tonight Shows with Johnny, in the 80's and eventually Jay, in the 90's. In 1985, we began shooting 125 half hours of our own Syndicated TV Series, Comedy Break with Mack and Jamie, hosting and
performing skits with such icons as Tom Poston, Fred Williard, Steve Allen, Ruth Buzzi, Julia Duffy, Mary Fran, Vanna White, Ellen DeGeneres, Sinbad, Paul Rieser, Kevin Pollak, and Jan Hooks. We were shooting the 60th show of our 125-
show run when two brothers from Detroit showed up at my office door. One of the
somewhat disheveled brothers said,
    "We love Comedy Break, and we've written some sketches for the show."
It was a godsend. We only had five writers, plus ourselves, and were shooting six half hour shows of original sketch comedy a week. The sketches and jokes these brothers handed to me were wonderfully funny! I took them to the producers, Viacom, and showed them the great material. They said,
    "We can't afford any more writers, tell them it's a "no." That's why I always refer to them as the Viacomese, sworn enemies of Comedy.
The next day I met the brothers, Mike and Brian for lunch and gave them the news that it was a "No." I asked them where they were living and they responded,
    "In our Delta 88."
    "Is that your apartment number?" I queried.
    "No, It's our Oldsmobile."
So, I offered to pay them $25. for jokes and $75. for sketches. They wrote great stuff for Comedy Break, as I happy ripped through a few checkbooks.
I'm glad that they were able to stay in L.A. because 25 years later, Brian Scully produced *Family Guy* and Mike Scully produced a little show called *The Simpsons*. Someone once said, "Comedy is a Funny Business," they were right.
One night long ago, after a set at Catch a Rising Star, yes, it was a "killer" set and we "slayed 'em." The co-owner of the club, Rick Newman, came up to us at the bar and lavished us with praise. He was Pat Benatar's manager, and he wanted to
manage us but Mack and I were such larval comedians, having been in the biz for six long months, we didn't pick up on his gushing evocations, even when he would invite us down to his private basement office to "party." We usually had a set
somewhere else that night and didn't have time to even get a whiff of the offering. The "Catch" stage was a very exclusive place and to get a set; one had to be invited by the M.C. of the evening. At the time the M.C.'s were David Saye, Richard
Belzer, and Bill Maher. Comics would perch at the bar hoping to be approached by one of these deities, who could launch careers with a mere "hello." One night, with no introductions necessary, Bill Maher said,
    "Hello."

All of the Comics at the bar leaned in a bit closer. He said that he heard we were "killing" at the Comic Strip and Improv. Would we like to do a set in 10 minutes when "Jerry" got off? We said something like,

"Sure, great, very cool, thanks, outstanding, terrific, wow Bill, thanks Bill, how much time?
"Can you do a funny 12?"

We assured him that we could, and as he walked away, he half turned and said, "Jamie and Mack, right?"

"No, Mack and Jamie, whatever Bill, don't worry about it we'll do a killer 12."
Immediately, we huddled and scribbled out our 12 minutes on a napkin.
Understand that comedy teams can't just get on stage and talk the funny for 12 minutes, because one has to know what the other is going to do or say and pick up their cues for the next "bit." We decided on Game Show, Paid Gig, Jean Claude
Boulon, Benihana, Bee Gees and Desperado, a great closer where Mack insisted on playing a romantic song and I resisted to the point that when he launched into Desperado, despite my protestations, I stood well behind him and tapped my face
with Scotch Tape. When I had transformed into a cross between a poorly wrapped
gift and a burn victim, the audience was doubled over as Mack, without apparent knowledge of my cellophane face wrap, said,

"Come on Jamie, sing the last verse with me."
I did and we brought down the house. I always loved acting that bit the over 3 thousand plus times we did it. We waited at the side of the showroom and watched
Jerry finish up with his "missing sock" bit and Bill, the consummate pro, introduced
us as "Mack and Jamie".
We bounded on to the stage, and as we passed Bill, he handed me a note that I surreptitiously scanned. It read, "Do 8." We would have to cut four minutes, and I had no way of letting Mack know as he was already in the middle of Game Show, a frenetic bit and somehow, during our banter, I said "Cut Paid Gig" enough times, through a broad smile, that Mack picked up on it and we went right into Jean
Claude and did that killer 8! When we took our bows and said "goodnight," our deity was nowhere to be seen. They were still cheering so we ran back up and said "goodnight," again, and we left the room as slowly as we could, still waving.
Walking back into the bar there was a flurry of activity at the club's front door. It was Bill Maher sprinting through the door, careening his way through the phalanx of party people in the bar. As he passed us, he blurted,

"8 minutes! NOBODY ever does just 8 minutes. I thought you'd do at least 12! Jesus, what were you thinking?!"
Well, we were thinking 8! He bounded onto the empty stage to face the silence of the lambs, he said something like;

"Sorry, I was powdering my nose."
Big Laugh. That was our first night of many to follow. Thanks, Bill. Now back to

Rick at the bar. He told us that one of the Eagles had been in the audience and wanted to meet us. Mack chimed in,

"Absolutely, bring him over!"

As he fantasized…was it Leroy Harris, Billy Campfield or maybe even Ron Jaworski! Suddenly through the crowded bar, a face appeared. It was Glenn Frey.

He walked toward us with his ever-so-cool rock star saunter and said,

"You Sons of Bitches! That is the purdiest song I ever wrote and now, thanks to you ass wipes, I'll never be able to sing it again without crackin' up! Let me buy you a drink or a dozen."

We hung with him at the bar until after midnight when he remembered that his date
was still in the showroom. He returned with the purdiest little cowgirl you ever saw
and leaned into us,

"Come hang with us tonight. I got a fully stocked limo, some party powder and nowhere to go. Let's find some fun!"

Setting out to find fun that night, we all belonged to the city. Feeling a little like celebrities, we went to a party that was in full swing or full rock. After a while, Mack
got nervous that his Mom might find out he was with models and celebs wallowing
in hard drugs and random sodomy, so he caught a cab to *Catch* and drove back to our apartment in Passaic. I hung with Glenn and Dixie all night and laughed purdy dern hard, making up our own lyrics to Eagles songs. 'Standin' on a corner in Winslow, Arizona I think I gotta' take a pee. It's a cop, my lord, in a Crown Vic Ford slowin' down to slap the cuffs on me." And so on. At 7:30 am, after a sumptuous breakfast, Glenn sprang for my room at the Warwick and we said our goodbyes, and hegave me a big bear hug grunting,

"Hey if you guys ever want to do that Desperado bit on one of those comedy shows, contact my publisher, and I'll waive the licensing fees."

He handed me his card. Three years later when we appeared on *Solid Gold*, they asked if we did any music? We told them we did Desperado, and they whined that
the fees would be too high. I called Glenn's publisher and the gal at the desk said,

"Oh, yes, of course, Glenn said that you might be calling."

Nicest guy in the world was Glenn. He could write a clean, mean song and he left millions with a peaceful, easy feeling. Sleep tight buddy…I'll do the same. But, for me I am fixin' to wake up tomorrow.

Sitting here, in this damn bed, watching T.V. I just saw an ad for the show, *Blackish* and am reminded that we toured with Diana Ross for five years and entertained audiences worldwide. Diana Ross's opening acts automatically become anonymous, as the only word on the marquee is Diana! We were the pickle that comes on the plate when all you really wanted was the sandwich. We had to prove ourselves every night. I must say that Miss Ross was a pleasure to work for. One

day she invited her entire orchestra, her entourage and her opening act over for brunch and a swim. I arrived early enough to help her scramble the eggs, flip the hash browns and burn the toast; while she still looked beautiful in her real hair! No

one brought bathing suits, so she sent my friend and one of my comedy mentors, Max Schaible to take everyone's size and style preference and get swimsuits for everyone. Max was apoplectic with joy at having been assigned a task by the Queen of Motown. She did have one big bugaboo. She was adamant about not changing anything in the show that was working, including OUR act! This was a five-year gig, and we would occasionally try out a new joke or bit that had been proven because it was working in the clubs. Whenever we did, we inevitably heard

that knock on the dressing room door. It was never Miss Ross. It was one of her daughters, usually Tracie. She would poke her head in and say,

"I saw your show tonight."

She was 14 and one of our biggest fans. She continued,

"I loved the new stuff but my Mom won't."

She didn't ever like "new stuff". Her motto, which she repeated to us regularly, "If it ain't broke, don't fix it" We dropped the "new stuff" the next show. Tracie now plays the role of the Mom on Blackish. The MOM! How old am I anyway! It has been particularly interesting for me, having been half of a performing partnership for over 35 years with how we each brought something unique to the process. Conflict, as in all comedy, was our creative spark. I was the liberal, vegetarian, optimistic, friendly guy and Mack was the southern conservative, carnivorous, pessimistic curmudgeon.

We were flying to Maui early one morning for a "corporate gig" at the Four Seasons Where we would live off of their Master Bill for four days, doing one show and splitting

$16K. As I stood in line, I heard a guy mumbling and grumbling over my shoulder. Without turning around, I said,

"Good Morning Mack."

"God Damn it" was the muffled retort.

"Mack, what's wrong now?"

"I've got a goddamn middle seat!"

I offered,

"Look on the bright side. Maybe we'll crash on take-off!"

Before all was laughed and done, Mack and Jamie had worked with some of the best in the business we call "Show." Tony Orlando, Bobby Hope, Lou Rawls, Leo Sayer, Michael McDonald, The Platters, The Four Tops, The Temptations, and

Diana
Ross. Forgive me, I know that it's tacky to drop names. Paul McCartney told me that.

One night we were hosting a corporate show for IBM at the Mandalay Bay in Las Vegas. Penn and Teller was the featured act. At the sound check, all they did was bicker and throw stuff. Later backstage Teller, the one who doesn't speak, pulled me aside and asked,

"How long have you guys been working together?"

I said, "Um, 30 years, how about you guys?"

"32 years. Don't you guys ever fight?"

After a second of consideration, I said,

"No, we really haven't argued in years."

He probed,

"How is that possible? How do you not fight?"

I said something that I'd never verbalized before, and didn't really, entirely mean, but it sounded apropos.

"We both realized, many years ago, that it's a waste of time to ever give a shit what the other one thinks."

A broad a flash of realization spread across is visage as he imagined the promise of better times to come.

A game show producer named Ronnie Greenberg saw our act one night and got the folks at Alan Landsberg Productions interested in giving us a T.V. series. We shot a little pilot for it with furniture and props from Ronnie's living room. One thing lead to another and before we knew it we were starring in *Comedy Break with Mack and Jamie*. We shot five shows every Saturday morning LIVE on TAPE with a studio audience. For each show we had guest stars like Steve Allen, Ruth Buzzi, John Laroquette, Julia Duffy, and we asked comic friends to come on and do 4 minutes. Many comics made their T.V. debuts on our show including Sinbad, Paul Reiser and Ellen DeGeneres. For 10 -weeks we endured this inhuman 50 show grind. Then, the show was picked up for 75 more shows but with a different format. Instead of hosting a clip show we were going to be doing an all sketch comedy show with two bright new stars Kevin Pollak and Jan Hooks. We had a blast but at the end of 75 shows, taping 6 shows a week with 5 writers, we were exhausted and the writers, who included Mack, were completely out of funny ink. We were called into the offices of Viacom, who produced our show, one morning. They were our benefactors and exerted their withered arm of comedic restrictions more than once. We called them "The Viacomese" because they were the enemy of humor. So, Toby Bryant, an amiable production lacky at Viacom tells us that they would like to do another season of the show. For some reason in my head, I thought, Oh, this is great I can buy a new house away from the cacophonous air ships that loomed overhead on Airlane Ave.

When we bought that house, we should have paid more attention to the name of the street. But I'll never complain… I've had a great life to this point because of the people

in it and as I lie here, I'm putting together my Life Book with mental images of each of

these people's faces and their impact on my life. My wife, Sarah is at the top of every

category but Mack certainly had a tremendous impact on my life and specifically my business life! We obviously had our ups and downs, coming close to splitting up many

times, over the 45 we performed. Imagine the classic scene of us literally yelling at each other as we were being introduced, then going out and doing a killer show! Well,

we did it! Did we hate each other when we broke up? Was there rancor and enmity when we split? Here's the log of our emails to each other when we both knew it was all over:

On Sep 18, 2013, at 11:08 AM, Ilene Walters wrote:
Hi Jamie. Hi Mack. May I please have your updated corporate fee and also availability for the morning of February 18, 2014 in San Antonio? The client is Pilot Flying J.
Please let me know if we may hold the date.
Thanks very much!
Ilene Walters - SpeakInc.

~~~

Sent: Wednesday, September 18, 2013 5:47 PM
Subject: Re: Checking February 18, 2014
Hi Ilene - thanks for thinking of us. Yes, we are available! We love San Antonio – our current rate is $8k (net) - plus two rd. trips (one from Louisville, Ky /one from LAX) - plus two rooms on site and $60.per diem per person (2). All subject to negotiation and we will guarantee a grand slam!
MACK & JAMIE
Clean Customized Comedy
http://www.mackandjamie.com

~~~

On Sep 18, 2013, at 7:59 PM, Mack Dryden wrote:

Hi Jamie,

We both knew this day was inevitable, but it still gives me a heart pang. I'm going to honor both of the holds we have on our calendar, i.e., Vicksburg and San Antonio, but I'm not going to take any more. We haven't worked since July of 2012, best I can tell, and once you've been off the stage for 14 months, I think the message from the world is pretty clear. I hope you're enjoying what you're doing as much as I'm enjoying what I'm doing. I'm on a roll that's very fulfilling and making me happy, and jerking myself out of that comfortable groove to rehearse an act that really should be just a historical artifact by now just doesn't appeal to me. In fact, it just makes me dread the work we'd have to do to remember it. I'm finally ready to close that amazing, colorful chapter with no regrets. For a couple of laid-forward, unbelievably incompatible knuckleheads who drove a beat-up Plymouth from Key West to NYC to LA, we did pretty damn well, I'd say. I hope one of these gigs comes through so we can do our swan song. If they don't, it was a helluva ride. Nobody really did what we did, and there's no way I could have done it without you.

  Cheers, Mack

<p style="text-align:center">~~~</p>

On Sep 18, 2013, at 9:16 PM, Jamie Alcroft wrote:
Ditto Mack - no way I could have done it without you. The "message from the world"
is because neither of us have put an ounce of effort into promoting Mack and Jamie
for a long time now. That is what is clear to me.
So, let's pass on both the dates even if they come through. It's nice to know that somebody wants us but I don't want to do it just for the money. We've had plenty of swan songs, let's just let it go and move on with whatever makes us the happiest.
Maybe that was part of the demise, that we just did it for the money for far too long. We both have found joy in what we are doing and that's a good place to land.
Wish we could have hit it big but we both made mistakes and then kinda' gave up.
C'est la vie! It was a hellofva' ride and a great career! As incompatible as you may
think we were, we (I) had some incredible experiences, both on stage and off, and

I feel blessed to have shared them with you and your family. We were an icon in the comedy team world and that will always feel good. Making a living for 35 years
bringing laughter to the world ain't a bad way to have lived. Success and happiness
to you in all you do. It's great to know you're out there. Funny, when someone asks
me "are you guys still together?" my answer will always be, "Always." Thanks for everything, onward! Jamie

<p style="text-align:center">~~~</p>

On Sep 19, 2013, at 7:43 AM, Mack Dryden wrote:

Jamie - Wow. Even I couldn't have predicted the grace and affection in your reply.

This is exactly the kind of mature and mutually respectful closure I was so hoping our Fade Out would be. I can't tell you how truly happy I am for you and your family
that your lives are full and exciting and fulfilling in the ways that matter. I think there's something special in the fact that we had a fine career together and then both segued to comfortable situations surrounded by people who love us and we love back, and that we both have nothing but affection and respect for each other.
In fact it's sad how unique we are in that regard.
I called Troy in Vicksburg last week thinking maybe hearing a voice might get some
action. He said there was a meeting on Friday and they should know something. Haven't heard from him. Since you're the one who was contacted by both Troy and
Ilene, I'll leave it to you to let them know we're declining.
Thanks for everything.
With sincere affection, Mack &

PS: I had knee surgery today and it went great. I hobbled back into the house on my own two feet. Amazing what they can do now. Hope your heart and overall health is good.

Does anything really start off innocently? Maybe an Adam Sandler movie but this was a long-ago night in New York City in another century. December 8th, 1980. An amazingly talented blues singer we knew from Key West was in NYC that night but she wouldn't sing until later. Imagine.

Mack and I had done our usual opening of the first show at the *Improv* on the west side and then went to the east side to do a middle spot at the Comic Strip then close the show right around the corner at *Catch a Rising Star*. We hung out at Catch to open the second show and then a middle spot at The Comic Strip, which was still around the corner. Finishing up with a drive back across Manhattan to close the show

at the Improv, usually going up around 2:45 A.M. between Gilbert Gottfried and Rita Rudner. That awful night we got to The Improv, for the first show, about 3 minutes before we were to go on. No parking spots, anywhere. We were larval comics then so, I started to panic and pulled Mack's arm off of the steering wheel and called out,

"There's a spot!"

"Where?"

"There, pull up in front of that Alfa!"

"The what?"

"That car with its top down."

".....the what?"

"The red convertible, stop, here! "

He stopped, confused. I hopped out of our car, and got behind the wheel of the Alfa. Mack almost pulled away fearing the impending grand theft auto indictment. I put the

Alfa in neutral and released the emergency brake, drifting back just enough for our car to fit in front. Mack parked. We ran the 30 feet to *The Improv* walking straight onto

the stage as Gilbert was introducing us in his halting and faux-angst ridden fashion. We got a standing ovation that night. As we walked out of the club, Mack said,

" Fuckin' incredible."

"Yah."

"Extraordinary"

"No, shit. They loved us."

"No, not them, this parking spot. How did you know to do that?"

"I learned on a stick," I explained.

"So did I!" He exclaimed.

"Yeah, but it was probably a tractor!"

The blues singer was Wendy Shirley, and she was in town to check out Mark McMillan

and his band; another Cayo Hueso refugee in Flagrant Talente. Somehow, we had all found New York around the same time. Frank Sinatra was singing *New York, New*

York and as I write, I'm listening to Snow Patrol's *Chasing Cars*. Each fill me with an audio-visceral memory of life's unpredictable moments. Thirty–one years of that joy was about to be stolen from me or, already had been from everyone. We met Wendy at TRAX for Mark's set. Wendy was a sweet girl and hearing her sing the blues so 'blue' made you wonder how such a girl, with barely a 400 grit, could have known anything about what she was singing. But, oh, right…she wasn't singing that night, at

least not yet. Listening to Mark and scanning the room, suddenly a beautiful blonde walked up to me. I've always loved that sensation.

"You look like him," she said.
I responded innocently, "only when I squint."
"No," she stopped me cold, hand to my chest. "You look like John Lennon."
Isn't it good knowing she would?
I launched into my dead-on impression of John.
"I only look like him when I'm fantasizing about you."
In that moment that she said, "You are creepy, he's dead you know. Somebody shot him."
Time simply washed away. There are events you wish hadn't happened in your lifetime: the JFK assassination, 9-11, Sandy Hook, the list goes on. They all leave me
with a profound feeling of guilt. I guess I must feel responsible for our flawed species.
Wendy and I set out to avenge the night and Mack came along. The scene at the Dakota was too morbid. I've never slowed down passing a car wreck. I always speed
up and light my votives later. We roamed the streets that night singing "Imagine" at the top of our lungs and in Wendy's case diaphragm. We sang and lamented until, just as the dawn was breaking, and the votives flickered, we were pelted with eggs from above. I guess our "sleepless egg chucker" hadn't read the news today, oh boy.

SUNDAY 9/24/17

I wish there was a better selection of channels in this room. I watched The Super Bowl in a bar, on a ship, in the Pacific Ocean, off the coast of Tahiti once. I was with a great group of folks who loved the Mack and Jamie show the night before...so they
must be great individuals, each and every one of them! It cost Cunard $50,000 to have the game shown in the bar. I made $14.00 in a pool. I saved what I wrote that night: *Luck is with me. I won $14.00, but I am losing an entire day. Make a note on my calendar we wouldn't have a Monday tomorrow because we crossed over the International Date Line...No Feb 5th for me this year...yet, I still have tomorrow, which*
will just be Tuesday....No one really understands it...they just explain it to you, give you a knowing nod and walk away. Maybe they knew where Feb. 5th has gone, and they just didn't want you to know. Hey if it's the International Date Line shouldn't you get one and not lose one?
Hello, People, of the Past. We just crossed the International Date Line on the QE2. We went from Super Bowl Sunday to what was going to be the day after tomorrow. This is my lost day, unrealized yet somehow peaceful and fulfilled in its lack of existence. I just had to take this opportunity to write from tomorrow to people who are
living yesterday. I don't get to do this every day, just on the ones that aren't. So, from
Tuesday, February 6th, to all those in Monday, February 5th, I bid you a long fondue.
Tomorrow has arrived before today ever came.
Like I said to myself just before midnight last night...."On Monday I'm going to finally..."
(then it was Tuesday) I shall remain in yesterday, until Wednesday. Still weird...it's 1:40 PM yesterday at home and 9:40 AM the next day, which is tomorrow here.
I just walked back to the ship from the internet cafe...about three blocks...everyone said hello, or "Bula" to me and I had a couple of pleasant conversations. Ever since the coup here in November...the town has been 'occupied' and devoid of tourists...the
QE2 was the first ship in since, and now the Amsterdam's in town and everyone is ebullient. This new ship, the Amsterdam, makes the QueerEye2 look like the Kon – Tiki. It's a beauty.
Yesterday, Mack and I rented a RAV4, Toyota, setting out to a place called Heavens
Edge and only made it about halfway before we had to turn around and go back. We
left at 8:30 AM and got back at 7PM....were able to put only about 170 miles on the car though, , thanks to the roads we took it over, I think it aged at least three years.
The women here, all look like George Foreman with an Afro, and a lot of the men look
like George Foreman with an Afro...as they age, they all seem to look alike! We'd had
a torrential downpour on Thursday night, so the roads were very muddy and deeply

102

puddled. Cattle, Scabby Teat Hounds, mongeese, horses and school children run freely along and across the roads. Every corrugated iron shack has the family sitting outside selling papaya, breadfruit or barbequing assorted meats and appendages. It's
not hard to imagine that there was cannibalism here until the 1920's. "Please pass the Larry" was often heard at the dinner table. Can you imagine?
Fellow writer, Sally Reno could, as she wrote:
"Please pass the Larry and give me some Moe
I'll have me those Curly Fries and a big cuppa Joe...."
We bogged down on a narrow dirt road because a herd of goats was in front of us. As we slowed, a small Nissan brimming with large Fijians flew past us on the right!

The goats scattered like lightning. I guessed that this might have been an ancient Fijian technique for gathering food. Later, a small group of blue and white uniformed school children were gathered around a young boy on a horse.... they flagged us down and asked if they could sing us a song? They sang a couple of sweet songs with their open faces beaming. They each asked for a dollar, and open hands shot through the window. We carefully drove off as they chased the car for at least a hundred yards. Later, we decided to turn around and re-maneuver through the kids as well as the "kids." Everybody we saw, waved "Bula" and then it started to rain...I mean a solid wall of water, for the next three hours, solid. As we persisted through the rain, we were surrounded on both sides by villages of people enjoying their "Friday
Night." The adults of the village all were playing volleyball in the downpour, and the young men were playing rugby in rag-tag fields that looked more like rice paddies than parks. People everywhere, smiling, walking in the rain and waving, "Bula, bula. Here comes the weekend!" Sons and daughters of former cannibals, happier than I've ever seen them! When we stopped in Sigaluva, we found a nice little Indian cafe....as we were paying our checks, in this chutney shack, the rickety old waitress approached and asked if we enjoyed the food...we said we'd loved it and then she asked in her broken Fijian/Hindi accent if either of us was married. I said I was and, ever reluctant to engage a stranger in a conversation Mack, clammed up. In the hanging silence, she offered herself to Mack in marriage. She said she was a great cook and needed an "American Friend." If Mack wasn't interested, maybe he knew of
an American who was in search of a friend. So not only did she offer herself to Mack but also, to any lonely person he might happen to know. She handed him a piece of paper that contained her name and number. She wasn't very attractive, but she apparently was very particular about her life-partner. Hey, she could whip up an "I'm Your Life Partner Curry" for anyone still breathing!

Even as a child, glued to the tube, watching *The Twilight Zone*, I recognized the plot was always driven by the same conceits; a person losing control of their surroundings,
then realizing they never had control in the first place. The expectation of regaining control is presumptuous, but adamantly, assumed by a delusional intellect. Their most
fervent wish is they will awaken, to an inexorable realization that they actually, are
awake and already resonating in a moment of genuine terror and revelation. Laying here for these 62 days, the vast wetlands between terror and revelation are becoming
wavy and mirage like. I don't have my organs yet. I must store up my terror for then.
My time now should be devoted to the revelation that I'm either going to stay or go.
Time to take a polar bear plunge into that deep mirror of reflection. Coincidentally, my
first revelations are all about terror; a youthful terror. Now a surrealistic form of mature,
or even elderly, terror creeps in from the crannies of my consciousness. In a few
minutes, they will prep me for the biggest unknown of my life.
Been waiting patiently, as a "patient" should for a Heart and a Liver for 62 days.
Reminiscing and conjuring those precious memories that preserve the experience of
living has been very cathartic which means it has given me a perspective and sense
of well-being. The Cardio Team wanted me to stay in the hospital until the organs arrived so that all they would have to do is roll my gurney into the elevator to pre-op.
Truth is there is no elevator involved but I'm soon to be on that gurney heading for
pre-op. They called tonight to say that they think they found a heart and a liver and
have dispatched the surgeons to Northern Cali with an empty cooler in hand. Crazy
thing is, I may be put to sleep and wake up with no new organs. Happens all the time.
Heart and Liver is "The Big One" so they want to get it right. I have a feeling there is
no small stuff in this transplant racket. This is sick but so am I right now. I can't help
imagining what my organs will look like. I've been exposed to organs at Thanksgiving,
thanks to giblets. When I "imagine organs," I remember the food in 1960's England
when I was a schoolboy. Blood Pudding, Steak and Kidney Pie, Shepard's Pie Ah,
yes, Shepherd's Pie, a fine example that English Cuisine is simply "a dare." I know
that the food has improved since the sixties otherwise UNICEF would be televising
appeals for aid, featuring emaciated English children with flies buzzing around their
sallow but still rosy-cheeked faces. Surely my vegetarian leanings must have started
then, as I had to pick through my food, sorting out the truncated valves and gooey
organs that had at one time functioned. Eating animal flesh was an accepted part of
being raised in a classically carnivorous American family of the 1960's. But eating
something soft and slimy that, at one time, had pumped and "functioned" within a
body was too damn graphic for me, especially now! Truth be known, I'm a
pescatarian. Have been for 47 years now. I love fish; I've just vowed not to eat

anything that blinks. Fish don't blink, why should they? Look where they live! I've shied away from meat since Wichita. I've read where every vegetarian saves 3,334 trees a year. That's about 156,698 trees that I've saved. When you multiply that by the 7 million vegetarians in the world, that's 1,096,866,000,000 trees. Hey, it's a start!

Somebody just knocked and walked into my room with a gurney. Here we go!

TUESDAY - 9/26/17

(No Entry) Slept, I guess…great dreams, I hope!

THURSDAY - 9/28/17

Slept more. Sarah and the kids were here and I remember hearing the

1812 Overture. Sarah brought a recording and played it for me. Can't believe I slept

through all 16 of those 18th Century Muzzle Loaded Cannons not to mention all of

those damn clarion bells!

So, even though this whole experience seems like one long, albeit blessed, hallucination, on Tuesday, just before I was put to sleep for my incoming trans organsmatron. A nurse leaned over me and said,
"How are you feeling Mr. Alcroft? Are you comfortable?"
"Yes, thank you."
She turned away, then turned back and repeated,
"Still comfy Mr. Alcroft?'
I said, with a mild impatience,
"I just told you, yes, thank you, I'm fine."
"Mr. Alcroft, that was 12 hours ago."
"You're kidding. I must have overslept."
"No sir, you have had a change of heart, oh, and we threw in a new liver too."
I was re-born through this experience in so many ways from top to bottom, from the inside out and roundabout. After a mere two months of waiting, a nurse calmly walked
into the room three nights ago and said that she had to prep me for pre-op. I got moderately excited and terrified. The word 'caveats' may not occur in the word 'transplantation' but believe me it is there. A few things have to happen. First, the organs are offered for donation from a "Donor Hospital." Submitted, in this case, from
a 46-year-old man in Northern California. My actual surgical transplant team all flew up to Tahoe, Eureka, or Yuba City, I like to think it was Tahoe, it's so pretty there! So,
they vet the organs and if they deem them acceptable, they remove them and "toss them in the cooler and haul-ass back here" as one of my more compassionate nurses
described it when she was wheeling me down to the OP, maneuvering as if she were
crossing three lanes to exit off the 405. Many of the recipients have traveled the same route and been anesthetized only to wake up with no new replacement parts. Mind you, they don't splay you open until they make sure that these previously enjoyed organs will be a good fit. Some of my "trans" brothers and sisters have woken up with their "old stuff." Returned to their rooms just in time to catch the last half of a rerun of Chicago Fire. My transplant team, with the generosity of a heart and liver donor who filled out his donor card, gave me a new lease on life; a lease whose monthly payments should be relatively easy, with a down payment of $2 million that was picked up by Medicare. Let's keep that program, shall we? Remember that guy who said that I would feel I'd be hit by a train, rather than a truck? Well, it is neither. Right now, I feel as if a meteorite has hit me. It didn't run me over or split me on the rails. It was apparently fired at close range. Thankfully, I'm still alive to feel this pain. Such a pleasure! So now that I'm 46 going on 70, I don't know whether to have a mid-life crisis or get a Reverse Mortgage..

Do you remember the cuttlefish bone that hung in your grandmother's parakeet cage? It was an elusive under-sea color known as sepia, touted to promote calmness and tranquility. Sepia is named after the rich pigment derived from the ink sac of the
common Sepia Cuttlefish. The word sepia is the Latinized form of the Greek σηπία. Yes, I looked it up.
In the silence, I saw a very clear image that I later realized was a video I must have been shown at some time along the way. In that video or somewhere in the literal or figurative ethers of Organ Swapping, I saw an aerial view of a pristine and calming beige/brown Grecian style temple. A solitary female figure sat, lotus legged, at the head of the temple. Suspended over the temple floor was a glowing cuttlefish bone floating horizontally about 3-4 feet off the marble floor. The female monk or shaman said,
   "James B. Alcroft, please breath in through your nose and then exhale through
   your mouth."
I did.
   "Once again, breath in through your nose and exhale through your mouth. Good, in
   through your nose and out through your mouth. Excellent, you are doing great.
Good, perfect, keep going. In through your nose and out through your mouth."
As she continued her chant, I followed her instructions. The frequency of her gentle request, became more rapid until, with each breath a bright yellow computer-generated band began forming over the floating monolith. With each repetition, the bands became denser and tighter until after three or four go-a-rounds, they collapsed,
morphing into the shape of my body, my corps, then my face. My guru's voice gently
sluiced through the void,
   "James B. Alcroft, are you ready to accept your new heart and liver"
I heard myself say,
   "Yes."
Her "Thank you" filled the void between death and rebirth, that will forever resonate within my deepest soul. I guess I had a choice between life and death. I wisely chose
the former. Then, that same silence.
My next memory, though quite vague, was waking up. It was three days later. I saw my family standing at the foot of my bed. My feet were sticking out from my sheets, good, no toe-tag! It felt like getting your parking validated.
   "Am I alive?"
They responded with the biggest smiles. They all looked like they had coat hangers in their mouths.
I deliriously shouted,
   "Konnichiwa Baby!"
Over and over until my nurse and doctor came in to calm me down. They pulled me away from the balcony from which I had been shouting Konnichiwa to a large partying

gaggle of friends and family gathered around the glistening turquoise pool below my three story high perch. Maybe my new heart was Japanese!? They may have thought

that I'd suddenly been overcome by a random attack of glossolalia, so they called in a doctor. When I was settled, I asked the doctor if I could get a copy of that video that

they had shown me just before my transplants. He replied,

  "What video was that?"

I gave him a thumbnail sketch, and he said,

  "No, I'm afraid not Mr. Alcroft.

I was truly crestfallen. He continued,

  "For you to get a copy of the video you describe would be impossible."

  "Why is that Doc?"

  "Why? Well…because, to my knowledge, no such video exists."

But I did see it, and I will forever take great comfort knowing that I will be able to watch

it always.

Comforted by the even greater knowledge, that even if no such video exists; I do.

'night.

Reading my previous entries, I realize how important remembering my life with my old heart is and how it all brought me to where I am, four days now, with a 46-year-old heart from Northern California. Images of my anonymous donor dying in an unfortunate variety of ways, will forever swirl through my mind as I continue to live by the grace of his compassion and generosity.

In 2014, My Dad was diagnosed with inoperable, untreatable, cancer by an Oncologist at the "World-Famous" UCLA Oncology Center last Christmas when he was visiting us in Cali. Within an hour of learning the news, he decided he had to get

his "affairs in order" so he went back to my sister's in Youngstown Ohio and sold his house in Pinehurst N.C. My sister took him to the "World-Famous" Cleveland Clinic where they confirmed he had inoperable, untreatable colon cancer. He decided to live out the time he had left in Youngstown, with my sister. One night they went to the

Boulevard Tavern where, as a family, we had always gone for Angelo Petrelli's amazing spaghetti, killer salad and on Fridays, we met our Catholic friends there for the best fried fish and laughs imaginable. They were sitting in a booth waiting for their

fish on this particular night and a guy walks up and says excuse me aren't you Jimmy

Alcroft, the golf pro at Squaw Creek Country Club? Dad said that yes, he was, and the guy told him that his Dad had caddied for my Dad on numerous occasions, and he thanked my Dad for his kindness to his Dad and all of the other caddies. He explained that he was Gregg Bogan and Dad remembered his Dad very well, and he

asked about him. Gregg said that his Dad had passed and then inquired as to what my Dad was doing back in Youngstown? Dad told him about his diagnosis and Gregg

told him that he was an Oncologist at the not so World-Famous North Side Hospital and that he wanted to see Dad that week.

Three weeks later, Dad had agreed to undergo a 4+ hour surgery and at 91 was Cancer Free. He has been golfing and enjoying life, traveling between my sister's houses in Ohio and New Jersey. The valuable lesson? Always get a third opinion. And always make sure you get it in a bar!

My father had an excellent reputation at Squaw Creek Country Club, the Jewish country club. My Uncle was the pro at the Mafioso Country Club, and my Grandfaither

was the Pro for 32 years at the WASP Country Club. The name Alcroft was golf in Youngstown Ohio and that made me very proud. I have a newspaper clipping from 1942 that reports when Bing Crosby appeared in Youngstown, he played a round of golf, the day after his show, with my Grandfaither. What the article doesn't tell you is that Bing and Grandpa were getting along so well that they both played the 19th hole brilliantly, sitting at the kitchen table in Grandpa's house and drinking 16-year-old

Royal Brachla Scotch. At the end of the evening and end of the bottle, Grandpa thought Bing was too sauced to drive. He called my Dad and had him drive Bing

back
to his hotel. Dad tried to get Bing to sing with him in the car, but ol' Ba-ba-ba-Bingo slept.
Sally Reno reports that in 1967 she was on her way my home for the holidays, from College when her plane made an unscheduled stop in Kansas City. One guy got on. He took off his hat and muffler and settled into the seat next to her. She's staring at him because he's Bing Crosby. He turns to her and says,
"Everybody's got to' be someplace."

Oh, there's Groucho…

I got distracted last night by an episode of *You Bet Your Life*, Groucho was the best improvisational host ever. Heck, I grew up on black and white television. Submitted for your approval, a decade landing smack in the middle of the last century, rife with burgeoning stardom, untimely death and a young boy's face illuminated by a cathode tube, courtesy of Philo T. Farnsworth. Jimmy Alcroft and Frank Valicenti carried a 58-pound Dumont 36'x 24' Royal Sovereign Television with a 15' Black & White screen, up three stories of stairs and wrestling with large metal rabbit ears, devoid of a large metal rabbit, to find a scratchy, snowy, signal from Pittsburgh, a scant forty miles away.

Betty White was a sexy ingénue, James Dean kissed off his youth in a Porsche in the
desert making a left turn in front of a pickup truck, and Howdy Doody was always strung out on something. The Grey & Grey, not quite yet "Black & White," pixilation of fifties mystification would render the *Twilight Zone* on Fridays, and *Lassie* then *The Ed Sullivan* Show on Sundays. The former resonating in the hollows of my imagination to this very moment and well beyond infinity. An infinity that, as far as I knew, might just go on forever. Submitted for your approval, Rod Serling was a chain-smoking, black suited, purveyor of surrealistic terror and futuristic fantasy that brings us to questions of our youth; when my source of visual captivation was in Black and White. My memories go way back before that 15-inch monochromatic screen. For example, I have a very clear vision of looking over padded cloth across the hood of a car, at the end of which was perched an orange light in the shape of a man's head and face. He stared intently into the night with the mysterious glow of enigmatic purpose. Following his gaze, there was a high, bright white screen, scored with thin horizontal black lines and symbols, that I later learned were words, as yet unrecognizable to my 3-year-old eyes. All of this was new to me, but I remember the sight, the texture of the padded cloth, the smell of my mother as I sat over her shoulder, I could hear the rumble and feel the vibration below my feet as I balanced eagerly on the edge of that classic's back seat.

One night at the family dinner, when I was around eight, I recounted a vivid memory of seeing a bright orange face, illuminated on the front of what I now knew was the hood of our Pontiac. Upon the telling, my parent's mouths dropped open in unison and closed simultaneously into disbelief. Mom offered,
 "There's that overactive imagination again. You couldn't possibly remember that."
 "Yeah," Dad chimed in,
 "That was the light on the hood of our '49 Pontiac. We sold that and got the station-
 wagon when you were…let's see…about 3 and a half."
Mom was suddenly uncomfortable.
 "Yes, honey, you must have just heard us talk about it. Now, eat your dinner."
 "No, I remember that light and that night, don't you?"
Dad stalled and stuttered,
 "Of course, son…but you couldn't possibly. Um, Ginny, are there any more stuffed
 peppers?"
 "Sure honey, I'm so glad you love my stuffed peppers."
Mom attempting a shift in the conversation,
 "How was work today, sweetheart?"

I persisted,

"I was looking over Mom's shoulder from the back seat. I could smell her perfume. The same stuff you wore when we went to Frank and Cass's last weekend. There was an orange Indian head on the front of a white hood and a movie theater down the street with a long word on it that started with "OK". We parked in front and went in."My mother acquiesced, only slightly,

"That must have been the night we saw Oklahoma at the Strand, but you were only

three and you always fell asleep in my arms before the movie started. Saved us a
fortune on babysitters, didn't it Jimmy?"

Dad concurred with a grunt and returned to his insistence,

"You couldn't remember that son; you were too young. We must have told you that
story though I barely remember it myself. Do you Ginny?"

"Well, I remember seeing Oklahoma, I love Gordon McCray, but I....um, let's see,
let me get you those peppers honey. Gravy?"

"You bet."

Thinking now, about this particular meal and the distant memory with which I had been blessed, or cursed. I can instantly be sitting in the back of Grandpa Morgan's 1952 Hudson Hornet, hanging on to the gray woven rope that hung across the back of the front seat. He sold the Hornet when I was 8. Then, he died from a heart attack when we were both too young. From the stories I heard, I wish I had known him better,

he sounded very cool. That '52 Hudson Hornet model held the land speed record for

a stock auto, sporting Twin H-Power. I knew he liked to drive fast because my mother

and grandma were always beseeching, yes 'beseeching,' in the biblical sense, for him

to 'please slow down.' He was a gunsmith who made some beautifully crafted rifles and he hunted rabbits. I always had an abundant supply of lucky rabbit feet that were

salted and still slightly bloodied. In the 1950's rabbit's feet, on small chains, were "good luck charms" for us, just not for the rabbits. He also rode a "Suicide Shift" Harley

that he tinkered with until he totaled the bike when he too, had a Widow-Maker. He was riding it away from a company picnic in 1957, waving over his shoulder at his cohorts, when his heart stopped in mid shift. He was 54, and I was 8. So much for those "lucky rabbit's feet."

TUESDAY - 10/3/17

Tom Petty died yesterday of heart failure. Makes me think about my Widow-Maker and how lucky I was to be the one in four that had symptoms. The day of my Cardiac Incident, my three children and I had been speeding "Hudson Style" in a rental car to Spokane, through color splashed Canadian farmlands, as we passed fleets of feather-festooned chicken lorries. Cluck yes, we were! Gleefully recounting the time we'd just spent with Sarah's parents, Hede & Nellie, We'd made sushi at home, fished in the lake, picked hundreds of ripe cherries off of their tree and looked through a scrapbook of Sarah's youth. Much was written about her in the Canadian papers and the kids got to see all of her trophies.

The 6-hour road trip only required seven stops at A&W Root Beer Stands, necessitating a mere 14 searches and rescues to restrooms of every possible variety.

Sarah had stayed behind for some "quiet time" with her folks for a couple of more days, so I was tasked with single-handed herding of our gang of three. With two children you can employ a man-to-man defense, with three you have to activate your zone coverage. Soon we were schlepping our luggage into the Spokane terminal.

Sarah and I had bought what we excitedly deemed to be a unique and very special salad bowl at an Amish settlement in B.C. and we had cushioned it carefully in one of our backpacks. Hayley "kinda' dropped" the backpack on the airport's unforgiving tile floor and the bowl shattered into hundreds of unique and very special pieces. I calmly dumped it out in a trashcan. For some curious reason, I noted to myself and my surprised tribe, I did not get angry. One of those vacation anomalies, I guess. We had a relaxing flight to Seattle. Sarah was flying on Delta from Kelowna B.C. and would meet us in LA in a few days. With a couple of hours to kill, we ate lunch. Sated and ambling toward our gate, there suddenly was a squadron of T.S.A.'s finest, decidedly over qualified quasi-soldiers, spanning the hallway to our gate. There had been some type of security breach and they, of course, were coiled and ready to spring into uncertain inaction, the way those crack T.S.A. agents do; having no idea what was going on but seizing upon any opportunity to create the illusion of having taken control. In moments, the breach had been broached and we were able to board. Thatcher sat next to me. Alysse and Hayley, were a couple of rows across, and ahead, of us. As we taxied down the runway an Eastern-European man and his son became a mildly irritating distraction, the boy was fussing in a Euro-child fashion, creating a Croatian cacophony of confusion. I suddenly felt an uncontrollable surge of nausea. Lousy timing for another bout of food poisoning. Damn those ravioli's, the Croatian irritant and the suppressed angst from that broken bowl! The plane picked up speed. Rather than throw up on, over and perhaps through the seat in front of me, I lurched toward the bathroom across the aisle and two seats over from the flight attendant who, though I was a scant three feet from her face, squawked into the intercom,

"Sir, please sit down! We may have to abort take-off, because of you!"

I felt no remorse. I looked up and saw her name tag thinking, only 'JOYCE,' fuck off or I may have to abort my lunch, just because of you. Bracing myself awkwardly within
the confines of the lavatory I stared intently into that three-megaton vacuum sucking Teflon hole, now in full puke position, entirely prepared to violently upchuck, the urge
quickly passed, and I realized that it had been only a fleeting wave of nausea. Returning, sheepishly, to my seat praising the gods that I had dodged that dreaded, and all too familiar, food poisoning. Wait! Not so fast! As the plane rose steeply, my body began gushing a torrent of cold sweat; simultaneously an enveloping pain rose from my core. Alysse looked back from her seat. She mouthed,

"Daddy, you're a funny color. What's wrong?"

Before I could respond, someone parked a Hummer H2 on my chest. It happened too
quickly for me to get their name or the number on their license plate. I was indeed having a Heart Attack with my 12-year-old son sitting next to me in 15B and my daughters two rows up in 13 D & E. Unfortunately, there is no lifeguard in the gene pool. I felt as if Rod Serling was standing at my side about to "toss" to a commercial. Instead it was "joyce," now in lower case. My grey face looked up, and I somehow found enough precious breath to say,

"I think I'm having a heart attack."

She cordially snapped,

"I doubt it, sir, you're just stressed about flying, happens all the time. I'll get you some
  oxygen."

As she turned, exuding all of the compassion of a Howard-Johnson's cocktail lounge
waitress at the end of a 14-hour shift, I halted her with all the voice I could muster,

"Wait, Joyce! I've flown over 2 million miles. I need a doctor Joyce, please."

To her credit, she sighed and reached for the intercom,

"If there is a doctor on board can you please identify yourself to one of the flight
  attendants?"

Good move Joyce! You saved my life. I didn't dare close my eyes. I darned not close
my eyes. I knew if I did, I would die and I couldn't do that to my kids. But right now, I'm in my empty room. The activity in the hallway is lulling me into a trance, I gotta' catch some zzz's.

There was, thank god, a paramedic on board and as I lay there on the rubber galley mat, absorbing the stale coffee, I overheard Joyce talking to the pilot. Struggling to make words out of what I was hearing, I caught the pilots voice crackling something about San Francisco. Joyce turned to the paramedic,

"Our pilot says we can be in San Francisco in 45 minutes."

"This guy's not gonna' make it for 45 minutes."

I took a deep breath and said what I thought might have been my last words,

"Portland!"

Miraculously the pilot heard me over the open channel and crackled,

"Well…uh…I can get us to Portland in 10 minutes."

Then over the loudspeaker, I heard,

"Ladies and Gentleman, this is your Captain speaking. We have a medical emergency on board and we will have to make an unscheduled landing in Portland.

Please make sure your seat belts are fastened. We will be descending as soon as everyone's in their seats with their seat belts securely fastened. We apologize for this

unscheduled stop, we'll be back on our way soon."

There was some kurphumphering among the passengers about not wanting to land in Portland, or anywhere other than L.A. and such. Whenever I hear the word Portland, whether I have said it or not, I harken back to that morning at LAX. I flew so

much in my touring days that for years my kids thought I was a baggage handler at LAX because that's where Sarah would drop me off for "work." One morning I was standing behind a man at the curb that had given his bags to an old African-American

baggage handler and proceeded to give the elderly gentleman a ridiculously hard time about 'moving faster' and being careful with his new bags. He stormed away without even tipping the guy. I was next and I said,

"Wow, that was brutal. What a jerk. I apologize on behalf of the entire human race and all of humanity that's ever lived, for the way that idiot spoke to you."

The old man smiled,

"Don't you worry about it none, I've seen worse.

"Well, that was unforgivable. I'm so sorry.

"Oh, don't mean nothin' sir, there's good folk, and then there's bad."

He tagged my bags and as I handed him a large tip his smile widened and he offered,

"Anyway, that man gonna' be flying to Portland, Oregon. Yes-sir, but those brand new bags…they gonna be flyin' to Portland Maine."

When we landed in Portland, Alaska Air took care of a taxi for the kids to the hospital and once at the hospital, Providence put up in the Doctors Quarters right across the

street. Just before I got into the ambulance the kids gathered around to tell me they loved me. I took my watch off my deadened left arm and handed it to Thatcher. In retrospect, how could I have expected a petrified 12-year-old to take my watch that now weighed at least 200 lbs.? Blindly, I tried to focus on Thatcher but instead saw

a
frightened 12-year-old boy, on his first day at an English Public Boy's School. As my vision blurred further, the plane and pain fell away. There was my mother sitting next

to me on an ancient wooden bench in a musky Great Hall, surrounded by glossy oil-portraits of past Head-Masters who had gazed vacantly across those dark and hallowed halls for centuries. Every eye glared through the shimmering canvases at that American mother and her son who were there to interview for the privilege of attending this bastion of British arrogance. As those long dead eyes penetrated the red velvet and darkly varnished shadows, I questioned; was I Oliver Twist or Pip? Was I strapped into 15A or fidgeting on that slippery and splintered wooden bench? Breaking the roar of silence and the fading jet engines, a swiftly moving cipher with great broad shoulders draped in a black pleated cape, flourished through the door, his eyes piercing through the feathers of his great horned owl eyebrows, drilling through my eyes, to the back of my skull. He didn't smile or reveal the slightest hint of humanity, rapidly blinking past the two of us, he pompously bellowed,
  "Allll-croft is it?"
He swirled and pivoted,
  "Follow me, if you would?"
We would, and did, follow his billowing cape through narrow antique doors of spun-lead glass, clicking the long-loosened parquet floors, as my three-year sentence at Bedford School foretold of my future in the past. Was I Freddie Bartholomew? Was I following Basil Rathbone? In my position, I might have been foolish to follow anyone over those ancient, clattering, parquet floors, where could he be leading me? Wherever it was, I chose to remain an idealist, assuming I would remember these vital sensations that someday I would surely be hard-pressed to remember. Who knows what medical horrors await my morning? Must sleep now.

THURSDAY - 10/5/17

Today was pretty mellow, other than the swirling fits of core aching agony, countered
by intermittent surges of the welcomed Holy Norco and Percocet bestowed relief.
All this stuff about England washes over me now because I've always believed it was
in that school where I learned that if you don't learn to face a little adversity you never
learn to cultivate resilience. I had assured myself that my parents had done their due
diligence, deeming that the best education in England was to be found at a Public
School, so named because it was an All-Boys Private School. Go figure. I quickly
predicted that this was to be how complex and perplexing these mounting tallies of
rarified Anglican anomalies might soon become.
We were living in the lesser of the two evil hotels in town; The Bridge. We would
remain there until we found a residence with central heating. Mind you, in 1960's
England central heating was yet to be imagined or engineered.
That first night we stayed at the Bridge, it must have been a Thursday, it was early in
September yet the cold pierced and stabbed through our bedclothes, impervious to
the seven electric space heaters that my mother had begged from the hotel staff. She
intermittently cried and cursed that night, wracked with the guilt of having brought her
three-hapless bewildered children, and recently widowed mother into a land that, at
that moment, seemed within spitting distance of the Arctic Circle! By the time the last
of the space heaters were plugged into the outlets I saw Terry, the bellman, wipe away
a tear or two as he made his way back to the lobby.
They had Americans stay in the hotel before but never Amedicans like this. Terry
was that sentimental and ever obliging bellman, who eventually became my best
audient, brought us tea and cold toast with even colder butter, every morning and
sneaked us sticky desserts from the dining room every night despite the all-knowing
eyes of Mrs. Marshall, the Front Desk manager. Terry was brilliant, he even got us
ice, in a country where they had apparently passed a law against it or someone had
merely lost the recipe. I was only 12, but I knew that a pint of Freon coursed
throughMiss Marshall's veins. Thinking back, we could have made ice after all! She
ran the front desk at the Bridge, and she exuded an ominous intimidation from her
perch behind that cage-like structure. You could be out of eyesight and earshot of
Miss Marshall and she knew exactly what you were up to and where you were up to
it. Had we not stayed in the Le Bridge for four months, so our centrally heated
house could be built. We might have bought some other house and had to snap up
every available electric space heater in the British Isles.

FRIDAY 10/6/17

I am a week with my new "equipment" and the pain has not so subtly increased throughout my core. I need to ride the Percocet express whenever I can as there are at least 90 sub-dermal stitches and even more metal staples on the surface in the

shape of a Mercedes Insignia, how Beverly Hills. When I look at it, I see a Peace Sign. Yes, I capitalized Peace Sign, there I did it again. Whenever I see that sign, I smile and am at peace. It is a symbol of my generation, life experiences. I strive for Peace in everything I do. I know you do too. Anyway, I'm cautioned to check the wounds for 'oozing,' but I can barely lower my head to see my staples. Whenever I hear or use the word 'Ooze,' I think again of those three surreal years in England and

the first three ultra-bizarro-surreal months at that Hotel. The Bridge Hotel was so named because it was adjacent to the only bridge in Bedford that spanned the lone river that ran through town. It was the river Ouse. If the word "primordial" comes to mind, hold that thought. Admittedly, the "Ouse" did meander oozily through town with

water the shimmering reflection of varnished teak, not the color one would expect of water anywhere outside of an abandoned Colorado mining camp. The murky brown hue was due, for the most part, to the proliferation of formerly ugly ducklings who prefer to be referred to as swans. In England, swans are a protected species because

they are "The Queen's Bird". The only animal there are more of than swans, are Corgis, The Queen's Dog. The Ouse smelled so severely of swan guano it made your

head snap back, the way your head does with the sudden scent of smelling salts, but

even snappier. It could only have been worse had the river been filled with hundreds of bloody Corgis paddling, floating, and pooping in the Ouse.

The only respite from the smell of the Ouse graced our olfactory senses was when the Bridge Hotel's headwaiter, John, would whisk by in the lobby or would grab his serving spoons to deliver over-cooked brussels sprouts or tasteless, long dead asparagus spears to our plates. I never liked the taste of asparagus but I always liked

the way it makes your pee smell. However, the smell of John would, as they say in Mississippi, 'Knock a dung-beetle off a cow pie.' It wasn't my grandfather's sweet Yardley or my other granddad's Old Spice. It was the harsh, stridently acidic smell of A greasy deep-fried English hotel kitchen. At least it wasn't Le Parfum de Swan or Eau de Corgi!

I do welcome the distraction this diary brings. Nightly, I am writhing in pain as I wrestle for comfort amongst my sweat-laden sheets. Unbeknownst to me, the tube they had pulled from my throat after I became a trans, bruised and scrapped my tongue to such

a degree that there is now a scab at the back of my tongue! Good to know. During my one of my sleepless nights in recovery, I hallucinated a spider and its web was perched at the back of my throat as I desperately tried to hold my tongue against my bottom teeth so I wouldn't swallow it, or god forbid it could have been bitten off by my

imaginary arachnoid. To compound my delirium, the machines in the room were bubbling like a cauldron. I felt like I was in a huge fish tank but how was my mouth so

dry, how was I breathing? My lips were so dry that when I tried to speak to the nurse,

they flapped at her as I did a perfect impression of Moms Mabley. Maybe I was Moms

Mabley? To recap, I was Moms Mabley underwater in a fish tank and there was a giant spider poised at the back of my mouth eager to eat my tongue hopefully before

I had the chance to swallow it and choke to death. Good times! The abject terror that

enveloped me was obviously not befitting the pluck of a Bedford Boy. What happened

to the cricket and football, boating and fives that were to have inured us to pain?

Where is Mamma Morphine when you need her? No more of that nonsense old chap!

Suck it up! Be advised, Allll-croft, you are being weaned!

I had become that Bedford Boy as every day I wore grey flannel pants, lined with cactus needles, a grey shirt, black tie, a much greyer V-neck wool sweater, with the greyest of all flannel suit jackets. My head was topped with a blue skullcap emblazoned with a proud eagle, the emblem of Bedford School.

"O'er north and south and east and west.
Wherever men roam o'er the earth's wide breast.
You'll find the boys of the eagle crest at Bedford by the river!
Now cricket and football, boating and fives and work by which men pay with their lives, 'tis ever
by these the old school thrives at Bedford by the river!"
(Repeat chorus)

What an imaginative chorus it was. I don't want to pay for" boating and fives" with my life. For a school that had been educating Earls, Dukes and the solicitors of the realm since Edward VI founded it in 1552, the lyrics were pretty damn elementary. John, not

Paul, Bunyan and left-handed cricket bowler, Alastair Cook were both alumni, so is James Biggerstaff Alcroft Jr. Those lyrics became etched in my mind, as every morning my father would drive me through the gold-gilded gates of Scholas Bedfordinasis. I have a solid mental image as if shot from a drone camera, of an eleven-year-old American boy from Ohio closing the door of his family's British racing green Jaguar MK II, as he turns reluctantly to endure the most remarkable three years of his life. Each morning, I filed into a row of the most straight-backed hardwood chairs this side of the electric ones at Leavenworth. The muffled laughter and the snide murmurings that bounced off of the vaulted ceiling was all because of me and my hair. The only crew cut that had ever graced this hallowed chapel.

"Bloody Yank, Amedican Arsehole, WOG!"

I understood everything except the last one,

'WOG". Golly, WOG, really?

The great horned Headmaster, Mr. Sutcliffe, whom I had met the very first day, presided over the chapel services, leading his flock in a tediously meandering rendition of *Jerusalem* by Sir Hubert Parry. I soon learned it was inspired by the words

of William Blake's short poem suggesting, "...and did those feet in ancient time walk on England's mountains green?" I have since learned that the poem was inspired by the apocryphal story that a young Jesus, accompanied by Joseph of Arimathea travelled to what is now England and visited during his pre-savior years, before he took on those 12 wacky publicists. I've always thought that everyone should see London before their crucifixion. The poem's theme, from the book of Revelation (3:12

and 21:2), describes a Second Coming wherein Jesus re-establishes Jerusalem in "Jolly 'Ol." The Church of England has always regarded Jerusalem as a metaphor for

heaven, a place of universal love and peace. So, Blake's lyrical queries in the poem merely imply that there may, or may not, have been a divine visit, when briefly there was a heaven in England. A heaven in England!? Jesus, Mary, and Joseph Cotton, how the hell did I miss that!? I never even got a postcard! I was raised on "Jesus loves me, yes I know," a lifelong assumption and comfort. I had no idea that the Prince of Peace had been educated in England as well. In those days before grey flannel, I hoped the Son of God's woolen robes had not been lined with exotic Middle-Eastern cacti. OMG, Four Weddings and a Funeral is on the tellie and they're singing "Jerusalem." Gotta' watch this.

In that movie last night, Hugh Grant lead, typically, with his eyebrows. As he delivered his patented quizzical expression, Andie MacDowell successfully kept up with everyone's overacting. I do like that fellow from "Room with a View," Simon Callow.

He probably attended an English Public School.

Sitting on an ancient long bench with five boys abreast. The desk had initials and slogans of the day, carved deeply by long deceased schoolboys. I remember, "Cromwell has Warts" and "Victoria Vagina". Ceramic inkpots nestled into the desks with quill pens and notebooks at each station. A Bunsen burner flickering at the front of the classroom and with no teacher, or master in sight just yet a boy with a bad haircut, it could have been Fraser- Holmes, Cook-Buckley, Hoof-in-Mouth, or anyone

of the hyphenated chaps in that classroom. Apparently, with all they are doing in medicine these days, hyphenation has become a mere "outpatient" procedure.

Anyway, the kid took the frozen inkpot out of my desk and walked it up front to be warmed in the burners soft glow. I involuntarily exhaled a cautious breath of joy through pursed lips. I thought it a true "hands across the water" gesture. He turned to me with the warmed white ceramic vessel feigning an awkward stutter step and spilling the warm dark blue-goo right at me. In true English-school-boy fashion, he missed. He "threw ink like a girl" as the archaic, highly inaccurate and inappropriate expression goes. In this case a more appropriate expression might be, 'He threw like

an English School Boy'. The warmed ink splashed onto the desk, as I instinctively countered by opening my legs wide, so it trickled between my grey flannels onto the ancient parquet, as it splashed, spackling my cactus-lined cuffs. He chortled an immediate,

"Sorry Yank."

My fellow students scrambled around me with great glee to assess the damage and a bell rang. Not a school bell, rather the ringing of the bell on the antique Raleigh ridden by, the equally antiqued, Mr. Squibb's. It's "ding-a-ling" grew louder as it rounded the classroom's bright blue door-frame. Instantly the chaps were back in their

seats sitting upright with their notebooks open. It was magical. No surprise there, after

all I was in a magical land where the Holy Lamb of God himself had trod on England's

pleasant pastures green. Mr. Squibbs parked his matte black 3-speed Raleigh in the hallway and walked into the classroom with all of the swiftness of one of those chameleons that moves forward and then back, then forward again, with stuttering steps on a seemingly unending, and far too fragile, twig. It took him forever to ascend

to his celestial pulpit that towered at least five feet over our heads. My notebook, covered with dark blue goo, was still not opened. Squibbs took it all in from his heavenly perch and muttered,

"Apparently…",

Speaking, with the halting effort of someone who had been recently diagnosed with

Early Onset Rigor Mortis.

"Apparently…chaps… our Amedican friend… needs another notebook. Who would
  like to fetch one for him?"

None of the guilty dared laugh or flinch. I barely smiled, but I did see Squibbs' eyes
shimmer with the faint acknowledgement of a joke, shared in silence. He was older
than the parquet, with a face as wrinkled as an elephant's ass, but I realized that
somehow, I had just become his "Amedican friend."

MONDAY 10/9/17

I started noticing Squibbie's curious curiosity with me, a week or so later. It may have been a fortnight, which is a favorite English expression referencing a unit of time of amounting to 14 days. It is used primarily to confuse the French. One day he summoned me to his lofty pulpit and asked,

"Allllcroft, tell me. if Amedicans spell the word twenty, t-w-e-e-n-y as you seem to

  pronounce it, do they spell thirty t-h-u-r-d-y?"

I assured him that we were faithful to the Queen's spelling even if we physiologically, had difficulty speaking her "English. Either he laughed, or he successfully dislodged an irritating obstruction from deep within his esophagus, He

did seem to enjoy the moment, whatever inspired it.

On Sundays, I would watch out of my hotel room window overlooking the picturesquely filthy alleyway that led to the Hotel's basement pub. Mr. Squibbs was

in the habit of riding his rustic Raleigh to "The Balls and Bullocks," or something like that, at around 12:30 p.m. knocking back a pint or two. I knew he must have seen me peering out of the window for on Monday's he would often say,

  "Did you have a productive Sunday, Allllcroft?"

I would respond,

  "Yes sir, thank you, sir."

To which he would cryptically retort,

  "You should get out more, George."

He called everyone "George." I liked Squibbie, and I liked Latin. Thanks to Squibbie, I know that sicat ambulans in platea quae erat ibi, means; "There she was just a walking down the street singin'." The familiar chant was: Latin is a language, as dead as dead can be, first it killed the Romans, and now it's killing me. After Latin was Divinity, sweet Jesus! Then came the infamous "Bun Break," an English Public-School tradition where warm milk and sugar-dusted, jelly filled buns are doled out to dirty knuckled, cacti flannelled blokes. During said break, one of them approached me with a friendly twinkle in his eye, asked where in Amedica I was from? I quickly scanned him and saw no recently warmed inkpots. As I started to say, "Ohi....".

He cold-cocked me. The boy behind me, on his hands and knees, broke my fall to

the gravel shards of the schoolyard. It was an old trick that got older with each cleverly disguised permutation. Sadly, I fell for various versions over the next three

days. Walking through town and The Bridge Lobby in various stages of swelling and discoloration. Mom was so outraged she threatened to storm into Parliament,

or better yet personally call JFK and have him order an air strike on the school, targeting the Bun Break coordinates.

TUESDAY 10/10/17

Every day my 'transplant team' stops by to ask me how I'm doing and all I can realistically say is,
   "I'm alive. I feel like I'm healing."
One of them always asks,
   "On a scale of one to ten, how's your pain level?"
I usually say seven, though after what I've experienced, pain has become so relative. I've been living with 25 since my "trans" so now even if it's 10, I say 7 and
move on to the next topic of discussion. There is one doctor on the team that is quite simply goofy looking. He's kind of a Mortimer Snerd with a stethoscope. I can't help but think that growing up he must have faced brutal ridicule, and he became a doctor, a transplant surgeon, a goofy gap-toothed conduit of life, He was
reminiscent of Terry, the gap-toothed bellman at the Bridge Hotel. Terry had a cockney accent so thick that Henry Higgins would have required a U.N. translator.
Sporting round bottle bottomed National Health issued glasses, eva' so rakishly. His teeth were badly stained, roguishly askew baby piano keys, spackled with something resembling Blue Cheese but he was the greatest ally any Yank had since Churchill, and he started to notice my incremental disfigurement and inquired
as to the cause? As I recounted my Bruising Bun Break Blues, he couldn't help but
suppress his crooked, smile; offering,
   "Those blokes aren't too keen on Yanks because of the war. You know; they 'ear
   all that war rubbish from their mums and dads!"
   "The war? What war? The Revolutionary War?"
   "Oh, no, THE BLOODY WAR!"
   "Oh, the "BLOODY" one, right! That's the one you're talking about. The last war that we had, of course, THE BLOODY ONE!"
   "That's the one!," Terry confirmed.
   "Of course, gotcha' matey!""
I guess it had only been 15 years since the Allies liberated Europe and there were
still a lot of resentments toward the way Yanks had behaved both on "England's pleasant pastures green" as well as on those horny British Birds, who might have been their mothers. Anyway, Terry was trying to help me understand this lingering
rancor and enmity, as I started telling him about my Masters. My French master was from the West End of London, so he dropped his r's. I gave Terry a sample,
   "Wegardez-vous la wive guache?"
Terry laughed out loud.
I persisted,
   "Wight then, Jacque allez à la bibliothèque dans la bloody voiture whiff Mr. DuPont an all!"

Then I told him about Mr. Titley, our history master, usually 'in his cups' by lunch when he would bombastically slur his words and most likely his facts. I did a slurred, sloppy impression of him and Terry laughed out loud, slapping his knee. My sisters and grandmother had been pulled in by the cackling, and now I had a crowd of space heaters and family in the room. I was on a roll, no cover, tip your waitress and try the kidneys. I did the stuttering and hyphenated Divinity Master, Mr. Griffin-Jones, The slobbering, sneering, Music Master Mr. Carroll and of course

the ancient, slooowmoving Mr. Sloth, wups, sorry, Squibbie.

"That's a bit of a laugh all right,"

Terry leaned into me,

"How do you get beat up so much when yer so bloody hilarious?"

Good point. By the middle of the next week, I had a strong five minutes for every Master. I'd post a trusty sentry by the classroom door while I launched into my latest Mastery of 'Master' mimicry. No more was I being hit; I was a "hit." At the

"Bridge" my Mom was still crying every day, and my mimicry did lift her spirits, which felt great. I also nailed an impression of a barely comprehendible Terry, the

front desk Nazi, Mrs. Marshall, and John, the headwaiter all of which sent Mom into fits of laughter, easing the tension while waiting for the English to figure out turn-of–the-20th-century heating technology. Living in the Bridge of Dystopia Hotel

in a rainy unnervingly cold, inhospitable country where the Lamb of God had probably ordered the lamb with a mint sauce, was a bit of hell if it hadn't been for bonding with my fellow "WOG," James Benson-Hall. He preferred to be called Beno. He lived in town, and we became fast friends as he spent many a weekend

at our house in the country. We had a quasi-tennis court out front and a wooded Spinney that became full of adventure. After I returned to the states it was sad that

Beno and I never wrote each other recounting the shouts of joy and whoops of delight as we flew through the wet-mud chill of the spinney on our bikes, sliding over ruts carved out between the wispy willows and lethal holly trees. No correspondence about the endless hours we fancied ourselves the as The Pacemakers, The Searchers, or The Beatles. Nor any mention of the camaraderie

we had as we bounced, obediently through those hallowed halls of Scholas Bedfordinasis, neither of us belonging and both of us knowing it. Still, for many years I had spoken of my friend in England, "Beno," as if we were still in touch. When I meet my soon-to-be wife, Sarah, I confided in her that it was one of the deep regrets of my life that I had lost touch with such a kindred spirit. That's when

a British Chat Show inadvertently became my facilitator by inviting two American Comedians on national television. We planned the appearance through our intrepid agent at William Morris and meet with the BBC writers before shooting the

show to set up Des with the laughs. Sheena Eaton was the other guest and was somewhat shit-faced, cursing at the make-up peeps. Des was drinking scotch out

of a coffee cup so, I figured what the hell! I turned to the on-air camera and said, "Hey, Beno, if you're out there, give me a call, I'm at the Conrad."
Hoping they would think that I was as drunk as they were and laugh it off. It was cut from the segment. I guess it wasn't that funny, though it seemed hilarious at the time, not! I set aside about two weeks and rented a car, re-visiting my old haunting grounds. It was my first time back in England since 1964. Twenty years later I escaped from London to Bedford, stopping at DuParys Ave and with a knock
on the familiar door I could almost imagine the exotic Argentinean Cuisine of boiling eyeballs and monkey brains wafting down the stairs from the upstairs kitchen. No response. Next was a drive to the Bedforninasis Campusius. The same old edifice draped in all of the lingering sensations of loathing, longing, and trepidation. I found the registry office and inquired about any records they might have of James Benson-Hall? They had no record of his forwarding address and thought he may have gone on to an Art School somewhere?"
"What about his brother, John?" I pressed.
Nothing. I think she said that he had left school for the Navy (it's been 32 years, I'm a bit foggy on that one). I was stumped, as the Yanks say. Frustrated, I wandered around the memory-rich campus for an hour or so hatching a plan. Returning to the registry, I asked if there was a record of all of the "Old Boys," pretending as if I were interested in any of the preening little prigs, other than James. The 'ol crone behind the counter offered that I could purchase a registry book for 30 pounds. Hell, my facilitator, Des, had paid me 8,000 quid for an appearance on the BBC, why not? I continued my journey of memories to our centrally heated house in Oakley, dubbed "Eagle's Rest." Homes in the English countryside had names in lieu of numbers. I visited the churchyard across the lane
and wandered down to the single lane Roman Bridge, replete with the semi-circle centurion stations. Walking up the hill from the bridge to the old windmill I tried to climb up to my old "perch," where I would enjoy adolescent meditations, but the stairs had rotted and collapsed. Alas, in the intervening years, there had been no Don Quixote de la Mancha to re-imagine this fallen dragon. I left these overwhelming, yet welcome, sensations and set out for Ayr, Scotland to be reunited with my dear old Aunties, Peggy and Agnes. I studied the registry in my spare moments and devised a rather ingenious plan. I would compose a letter indicating that I was about to embark upon writing a screenplay, depicting my halcyon days at Bedford School. It would be a sweeping, epic film to rival "Good-bye Mr. Chips" and "If," eschewing the gut-wrenching pathos and automatic weaponry. The screenplay would recount everyone's antics and efforts to survive under the oppressive bamboo switches of the tremendous horned fascist himself, Mr. Sutcliffe. I put together a mailing list of all the lads that I could remember, the Browns, the Gordons, the Watson-Lees, and the Garten-Springers; who both went
on to become a favorite breed of hunting dog. I sent out 40 letters and hoped for a
response to the "P.S." I put at the end of each letter, "Do you have any idea of the
whereabouts of James Benson-Hall?" Over the next three or four months, I

received return letters from over 20 blokes, lovely letters. Okay, they may not have
been total prigs after all. No one had any idea what happened to Beno. How could
this guy disappear, was he lying in a gutter somewhere clutching a can of Tetley's
Bitters, crooning "O'er north and south and east and west, you'll find the boys of
the Eagle's Crest from Bedford by the river...."? Tell me no.
Meanwhile...in another part of London...James' sister, Sarah, was traveling home
by train and happened upon a letter that had been placed in the Op-Ed section of
the London Times by one of the editors, a former prig to whom I had sent a letter.
I suppose he thought the idea of a Bedford School film fascinating.
My phone rang in California.
  "Hello?"
  "Hallo Jamie?"
  "Yes."
  "It's James. My sister, Sarah, read a letter in the London Times yesterday"
For the second time in my life, the re-imagining of a great friendship began. Within
a year, I was back in London for another spot with Des. This time, James and Sue
and the kids came to the taping and afterward we had a smashing Tea and Scotch
party in my Suite in the Conrad. We spent as much time at their house and in parks
and pubs as possible having a fantastic visit, picking up where we left off, learning
that through the lapse of time we had always been friends. Even in the vacuum
of communication I had regaled my Sarah with tales of my great friend in England,
whilst all the while James had been telling Sue of me and our antics. He was an
exchange student for a year in Princeton and had driven 16 hours. round trip, to
Ohio in search of the Alcroft Homestead. Alas, we were in New Jersey or god
knows where, at the time! Since then James and Sue have visited us in California
and my family. After the visit they wanted to drive up the coast to San Francisco in
a rental car. I made sure that they got a yellow Camaro convertible!

Pumping hard,
Squeezing grips
Pulling on cold metal pipes
Soft leather reins
Guiding with hips
Pounding pedals hard
Piercing cold air
Skidding through mud

Icy wafers sluice wild.
Faking fast and
Flying with the tires
Ducking the branches
snapping at my ears
It brushes my head,
And tears at my gut
Then turns me on point
To glimpse 'round sparse trees.
The smells and light through branches
Faces flash from the top of that double-decker
In the diesel driven whoosh of wonder,
I see each face through
Limbs whipping past their darting eyes
Finding the boy coursing the track
Clearer now than then,
Scarier then than now
Rich dirt, cleansed,
Worn complete through

My Spinney of '62.

WEDNESDAY 10/11/17

The whole family visited today, not actually 'whole' but in clusters. Alysse and Hayley came, to visit, first and I was able to deliver a speech to them that I composed while hallucinating that I was a dry-mouthed, toothless Sea Bass, resembling Moms Mabley, who was living in a loudly bubbling fish tank. I hadn't slept in four nights despite massive doses of pain and sleep meds. One night I was in an old-fashioned Western hotel room with gas lamps and wind-blown gossamer curtains. That's the night I thought I was having a heart attack as I was experiencing intense pressure on my chest. It was only when I screamed for the nurse that she said,

"Mr. Alcroft, quiet, please, we have other patients here!"

I told her about the chest pressure, and she explained that she gave me a medicine that creates pressure on my chest so I can sleep. Not!

One of the nights, in hopes of lulling myself into at least a quasi-snooze, I went through images of every Album Cover art that I had ever known. I saw the first Santana album, Buffalo Springfield, Cat's *Mona Bone Jakon*, all of the Beatles' covers, *Strange Days*, Dave Mason's triple fold, *Alone Together*, replete with the lingering seeds and stems. I visualized until dawn.

Shortly, or, a longtime afterwards, the girls were there. I asked them to sit down and launched into my prepared speech.

"Great to see my lovely girls, I love you both sooo much! We will have lots of great
stories to tell each other but before we do let's get serious. I wanted you both to try
and imagine that I have, in the last week, felt more pain than I previously ever
thought possible. I have suffered my first homegrown taste of agony as I
hallucinated, writhing on the floor, regretting each and every one of the free
cocktails
I said 'yes' to at all of the Comedy Club bars in my 30 years on the road. After the
shows, everybody wanted to be your friend so they bought you drinks, assuming
you would be even funnier with each round. As a result, I became an alcoholic, I
probably always was one. I'm not at all proud that I'm an alcoholic. Neither am I
proud that my mother was an alcoholic, as was her father. Not happy that my father
was an alcoholic as was his Faither, his two brothers, and their grandfather,
though
I never knew great grandad Harry, I remember laughing at family gatherings
hearing
that his favorite expression was 'Well I'll not say no if you're buyin'! I assume he
was
one too. The bottom line is that I never want you to ever, ever, suffer as I have.
Please promise me that you will always so 'No' to another drink and never be an
alcoholic."

"We promise Daddy."

THURSDAY 10/12/17

I gave the same speech to Thatcher this morning and he said, "I promise Dad." One Sunday, in High School, my three buddies and I were flopped on the sofa, bored out of our minds. So, my friend, Randy, stole a large Colt 45 Malt liqueur from his family's fridge, and we all split it. It was the first time I'd drunk Malt Liquor ever and within minutes I was the drunkest I'd ever been in my life. Alcoholism is hereditary….so it's relative, right? There is no life guard in the gene pool. We were high, High School sophomores, high and wise fools. I decided to use my talents or at least exorcise my mean-spirited side to call our neighbor Cathy Marshall. She was president of the New Jersey Beatles Fan Club. It was the sixties. It was one of those ultramodern princess phones. It took forever to dial a number on that thing. I remember thinking, why did the emergency number have a nine in it? Here's how the call went:

"Hello"?

My best Brian Epstein.

"Hello is this Cathy Marshall of Morristown New
Jersey?"

"Um Yes, it is…"

IT WAS CATHY!

"Cathy, I have some brilliant news for you…you have been chosen out of all the presidents of Beatles Fan Clubs across America to be spoken to by one of the
Beatles…we have John Lennon and George Harrison standing by in London to
have a chat with you…who would you like to speak with?"

"Oh, my god…you better talk to my Dad. He's from Albania"

I thought she said Alabama, so I was ready to speak to a good ol'boy and tell him I was happier than a cat on a liver wagon to make his acquaintance. But wait…I had to convince him I was Brian Epstein.

"Hullo?"

"Yes hello Mr. Marshall, this is Brian Epstein, I manage a singing group called the
Beatles."

"Beagles?"

"No….yes the Beagles and your daughter is about to speak to one of the, um,
Beagles all the way from London, England."

"This for real?"

"Yes, I assure you this for real."

"For real?"

Absolutely, and it's all for Cathy!'

To his daughter,

"It's for you!"

"Hello"

"Yes, hello again Cathy…to which of the Beatles would you like to speak?

"Um, oh my god, John…John Lennon."

"Right then let me just patch you through."

I did my spot-on John Lennon.

"Hello, it's John."

"Oh my God!"

"Well not quite, they say I might be his son."

"Excuse me?"

"Never mind, how are you love…."

"Oh, my gawd!"

"Listen Luv; we've got this new film cuming out, cha' know. It's called HELP! It would

be fab if you tell your mates that we called to say hallo and maybe you all could go see the movie."

"I will, I will. Oh, my GAWD!"

My buddies and I had a huge laugh about this, and by the end of the call we had all sobered up. The next day I went to school and took great delight in hearing Cathy tell all her friends about talking with John. I let her have her moment. At the end of the day when I got off the school bus, I went into Gaebel's Drug Store to get my usual Birch Beer and Ring Ding.

Mr. Gaebel said,

"Hey Jamie how about that gal in your neighborhood yesterday, Cathy Marshall. She got called by one of those Beatles!"

I was stunned. Nay, petrified.

"How'd you find out about that?"

"Right here in the paper…Front Page"

There it was on the front page of the Morris Daily Record, "Local Girl Gets Call From Beatle." Was it too late to scour the city and destroy every newspaper? I guess so…I took my Birch Beer and Ring Ding and started to walk home in a daze. Was that day a Thursday? I was closer to the ocean now, I could jump a tramp steamer. How long could I live on a Birch Beer and Ring Ding? I knew my dad would know it was me. I knew there would be a price to pay. Dinner was very tense that night. I finally broke the silence with, as John,

"How was work today, Dad?"

"We'll probably get sued and lose the God Damned house to some shaggy haired English son of a bitch! You, young man, are grounded for good. Go to your room"

That was the end of it. I did confront Cathy Marshall on the bus and I told her, as John,

"Cathy, it was me that day don't cha' know, I was John Lennon."

"No sir Jamie Alcroft, that was John Lennon, I'm the one who talked to him, not you!"

"Precisely."

"I know it was!"

"It bloody well wasn't."

"Yes, it was, just ask my Dad!"

I still have the clipping, and she probably does too. I think about the fact that she's out there somewhere, telling her grandchildren about the day she got called by John Lennon. But was it really John? In her heart, she'll never really know for sure but I hope she believes that it was. Life's more fun that way.

Years later Ron Maranian called me in NYC at 1 A.M. and said that he had a night late call-in show and no one was calling in! So, I called him as John Lennon. We chatted up the ruse for quite a while and he got another call. The guy sounded like, and said he was, John Lennon. But was it really John? I don't know. He was really good and he had an accomplice. I heard a woman with a high-pitched voice calling out in the background, "Come to bed John!" In my heart, I'll never really know for sure.

Well, I'd better go. I'm still grounded and if my Dad finds out I sneaked out of the house to get a heart transplant; he'll kill me!

A time for reflection as I break in this 46-year-old heart. It has become very apparent that I had twice as many visitors when I was dying as I do now that I am expected to live. Did I mention that it was only after I was christened The Tinman by friends Bob Rang and Michael Villegas, that I found out one of my transplant surgeons was Dr. Todo. Todo, "Toto," really? I was relieved that the woman at the top of the Temple did not use my full name when she revived me. She was calm and soothing throughout
and within that heavenly silence I inwardly thanked her for not saying my middle name. Also, relieved that when I checked into emergency lo' those 49 days ago that I didn't give the gal behind the security glass my full name. James Biggerstaff Alcroft Jr. My sophomore year of High School, in New Jersey, I was mortified when a friend,
Carl Vom Eigen who had earlier that day been "helping" in the school office and had stolen a peek at my records. It was right after lunch, on a Thursday and I was trying to impress a leggy cheerleader, who sported the cutest tush this side of "The Ice Capades." with the fact that I would be "rockin' out" as Conrad Birdie in the upcoming
school play and that I could get her free tickets. Hell, everyone could get free tickets. Suddenly the words,
"HEY BIGGERSTAFF," echoed…echoed… echoed down the halls. For a guy who would someday become a very wise Presbyterian Minister, Carl had a bit of a mischievous streak about him. My suspicions were confirmed one Sunday when he and another friend, Brian, were bombing through post thunder showered Morris Plains, N.J. in Carl's '59 VW bug and as they passed under the Erie Lackawanna R.R. overpass, through a huge puddle, they discovered that there was a hole in the back-seat transmission hump that sent a geyser of fetid oil-soaked rainwater shooting
up to, and almost through, the headliner. They immediately detoured to my house, knowing I would be up for a ride. They also knew that I loved to ride in the middle of Carl's back seat, hanging orangutan style from the hand straps on each side. I unwittingly positioned myself perfectly in the middle; as the underpass puddle approached, more accurately, as we approached the puddle, the front seat conspirators started giggling uncontrollably. I unwisely joined in, rearing my head back
in mouth wide open laughter just as Old Faithful caught the roof of my mouth with the
singular force of a fire-hose. Now that's funny! It took a week for me to completely dislodge a piece of Carvel Ice Cream Wrapper from my adenoidal cavity. Chocolate Praline Pecan, 30 wt. as I recall. Think the NORCO is starting to kick in and reduce my pain to a whopping 6! Just today, after I thought most of the pain and "a little pressure" had started to ebb, there appeared a troll like creature at my door. She was
more like a munchkin who perhaps had chosen to be true to my "Tinman" theme. I must say it was one of the most vivid hallucinations to date, rivaling Mom's Mabley in

134

the fish tank! My Munchkin was female and was wearing a white Dr.'s coat. My nurse
was unbuttoning my pajama top at the time and said,
 "This is Doctor Restivo. She is an expert on post-op drainage, and she's here to
  take out your last tube."
That was a sentence loaded with closure. Okay, I've had tubes removed before, easy-
peasy. Dr. Restivo introduced herself and explained her suddenly escalating bizarre
behavior, as her small frame climbed on top of me, deftly straddling my
torso. She began to speak from her "superior position," but, I stopped her,
 "I know. I'm going to feel a little pressure, right?"
 "Oh no, it's not pressure."
With that, she yanked, yes yanked, a 12-inch tube from my chest and as it reluctantly
emerged, I watched in horror as a tell-tale trail of my blood splattered across the
ceiling directly over my head. I observed this with such disbelief and horror that I felt
nothing.

I have since learned of the origin of my unnervingly odd middle moniker. In 1922 my grandfather, Albert Edward Alcroft, was the assistant pro at Belleisle Country Club in
Ayr, Scotland. As was the tradition, a Dunlop Club Salesman, who knew he would probably sell some clubs today, wanted to play the fabled Course and my grandfaither, Albert, the assistant pro, obliged. After 18 holes Al had set the course record with a 63. A year later that same Dunlop Salesman was plying his putters at Youngstown Country Club in Ohio. His target audience, the pro was visibly agitated because his assistant pro had just taken a late-night train to Niagara Falls with the daughter of one of their most prestigious board members for a quick "ride in the barrel." The salesman, one James Biggerstaff from Schenectady New York, told the irate pro about this young Scot who broke the course record at Belleisle. The pro sent
for my granddad and six months later James Biggerstaff Alcroft Sr. was born. Within the next two years, the whole family was in my birthplace, Youngstown, Ohio.
Youngstown, Ohio, in the mid 50's, was a teamster ridden steel town in the Rust Belt
of Ohio. I have so many vivid childhood memories, of going to Lake Erie and snorkeling for re-treads. Another is roasting marshmallows along the banks of the "flaming" Cuyahoga River. The only river since Biblical Times or even Greek Mythology that has ever actually caught on fire!
I miss those magical, sticky, watermelon'ed and salty summer nights of oppressive humidity and Capture the Flag. Weaving, running hard and dripping, through the magical flutter-by of fireflies that were summarily sacrificed as white man's war-paint. We "whooped" shrieks of primal aggression, as we streaked the still glowing ass ends
of those fluttering yet doomed, 'lightning bugs' on our gleefully festooned and glistening faces. Grandpa Morgan, of speeding Hudson fame, pulled me aside one night, during a break from a raucous whiskey driven game of Canasta, and imparted this gem of wisdom,

"Remember Jimbo-Jambo-Jamebo; you might think someone has their head up their ass but believe me, Bub, it's cleaner that living in Erie."
My mother often scolded him for those outbursts of random whiskey wisdom. He thought we were out of her earshot. But, come on, she was the mother of three and aurally omnipotent!

SUNDAY 10/15/17

For the last few weeks, I've been visited by what seems to be the entire Physio-Therapy roster here at Cedars. The first ones to visit had me wiggle my toes and raise
my arms above my head, no easy task with this two-week-old Mercedes scar. Though
I prefer to think of it as a "Peace Sign". I guess I could have ended up with a Hyundai
or an Acura, worse yet a Volkswagen! My PT coach is this high powered, super energetic and overly effusive Aussie named Janet who has me up and down and challenges me to walk just a little more every day. We've struck a happy antagonism between us, and it seems to be working. I actually enjoy her personality. My Lung Doctor, Dr. Levin is a hoot. A very funny guy when he's relaxed and a very serious practitioner when he gets down to business, an admirable combination. He's the kinda' guy who I'd hang with. Anyway, back to Janet. She gets me up and walking more and more every time. Today she told me that if I could make it down the hall and back that she would recommend my discharge tomorrow! She challenged me to make it to the little green EXIT sign at first. Then she would have them pick me up in a wheelchair. Soon, she would get me to the exit sign and back, then the entire hallway…and back. (My challenge for discharge. Don't know how I did it but I wanted to be home, so badly that I did that long haul twice. Later in the afternoon, Dr. Xie, my guardian angel from the transplant team, who plead my case, stopped by and said that she had met with the Liver team, the heart team and had just read the report from my favorite Aussie. She didn't see any reason why I couldn't go home tomorrow. I'm loving that Aussie! I remember the first time Mack and I went to Sydney to do a show. The flight was unbearably long, so I hung with the Stews in the galley for a bit of a party in my drinking days. At Customs they asked if I had a criminal record? I said,
   "Really, I didn't know I still needed one!"
There was a slight delay at customs.

MONDAY 10/16/17

They "Released," "Discharged," and "Expunged," me today! I'm in a daze but free! Free at last! Konichiwa Baby! I decided to have a bit of fun. They require you to leave the hospital in a wheelchair pushed by an attendant. I wrapped a blanket like swaddling around a newborn baby. I caressed it in my arms, cooing and awing at the
empty blanket in my arms. I got a lot of confused reactions, well worth the trouble and
a great piece of acting if I do say so myself.

TUESDAY 10/17/17

Arrived, a bit shaky, to our new apartment yesterday. While I was undergoing my "bad dream" with the excellent outcome, my soul mate for life was moving us from Thousand Oaks (one hour plus from Cedars) to a new place in Valley Village (about 20 minutes from Cedars). It's a spacious apartment and will serve us well, as I will return to Cedars, at least three times a week. My sisters bought me a Barcalounger chair, and I don't know if I'll ever get out of it! I'm back and forth from the chair to the bed and already questioning whether I left the hospital too soon. Still sleeping on my back because of the staples on my outside and the stiches on my inside. I yearn for the time when I can sleep on my side again. I am required to down nineteen pills for the morning, one at noon, eleven in the evening and seven for bedtime. I think it was Volunteer Bill who told me I'd have to take about 50 pills a day…out, out damn Bill. I have to meticulously record my blood sugar, weight, pulse temperature and blood pressure three times a day. For now, I have to exercise for 30 minutes per day which shall increase in time. I'm wondering how I will ever find the time to schedule my visits to the "Tinkletorium"? Nevertheless, I am home. I've made multiple deals with the Devil and God, as well as his alleged son, and all who might have had any influence per my release from Cedars. I know that it was a lot of me who did it. Hell, I was doing at least 5 shows a day for the Doctors, Nurses and Physical Therapists who stopped by. My attitude from the start was that I assumed I was dying, as I might have been. Okay, I was. And I was going to have and get as many laughs as I could while drawing breath. As I said, I know that my tactics were a significant factor in getting past the dual transplant age limit and getting home but am I here too early? We shall see. One of my more attractive Doctors told me, after the rest of the team had left the room, that she loved seeing me on her rounds. She said that I always seemed to be able to elevate the mundane. That has stuck with me and I will aspire to the accolade as much as my current pain will allow. I have voluntarily subjected myself to pain in my life for the sake of recreation and ofttimes peer pressure. Whether it be running a finger through a flame, seeing how long you can hold your breath underwater, listening to your smelly great aunt tell stories or, as in my case, playing rugby. Our Bedford School rugby games were never postponed due to bad weather; rather they were played DUE to lousy weather. My Latin friend, Mr. Squibbs, was our coach and with his knowledge of Roman battle tactics, he channeled Caesar when it came to game plans and time-honored, battleground tested, conquering strategies. He would line us up before the game, and randomly check us making sure we weren't wearing anything under our shorts like the 'Spartans' we were expected to be. Nothing! Nada, Zilch, Zip! Ball Buster Bupkes. Before your imagination runs wild and post-mortem molestation charges are filed against ol' Squibbie. He used a mirror on
the end of a stick and it WAS school policy. Remember "work by which men pay with
their lives"? Rugby fell into that category. I became the secret weapon, not because
I
did impressions on the playing field, though I did, but because I could pass the Rugby
ball like an Amedican football, twenny or sometimes thurdy feet! In the fordy plus years that have passed since those passes in Bedford, many Rugby players now

pass like "the Yanks". But I might have been the first. We would play until the mud was caked on in layers and return to the locker room to bathe. Yes, bathe, as there were no showers. "Showers" were reserved for April days in song alone. We would plant our muddied sweaty, naked bodies into a common bathtub, all fifteen of us. Even if you were third or fourth in the tub, it was like slipping into a mud wallow with a clamoring herd of Wildebeests, ever expecting African Crocs to pull us down the muddied banks to a migratory death. I ran hard on those muddied fields of glory, but I always saved my most ardent sprint for the race back to the locker room so that I could be the first into the temporarily fresh water of that communal tub. I ran like the wind!

WEDNESDAY 10/18/17

This morning, I laid in our bed for as long as my laid forward self would allow. I slowly got up, using the lateral elbow trust they taught me in Phys. Therapy. I was home for Christ Sake, I had to move around, but I didn't have to get dressed, did I? Truth be known, I'm still in my pajamas. I've allowed myself that today, what the hell? I won't walk Henry today…we're on the third floor, but there is an elevator. My problem is, I don't know if I can make it to the elevator! We moved here so we could be closer to Cedars. The hour-plus trip from Thousand Oaks was too much to expect when we had no idea what to expect. I just stand on the balcony and revel in the outdoors. Everything is music to my ears and a feast for the eyes. 85 days is a long time to yearn for fresh air, birds singing, and the sounds of traffic. I draw the line at garbage trucks backing up. Sounds too much like an I.V. running low. An innocent coincidence occurs.

It's been a journey that shall be never-ending, and my lessons are yet to be learned and absorbed into whatever life remains. Alysse, the Elder, will be married to her soulmate, Jack Mullins, in June of 2018. She is the sweetest most sensible person that I know. She is much older and wiser than I will ever be. I'll live to walk her down the aisle in June of 2018. My middle child Hayley is a force of nature. A film and television actress she's a songwriter, a screenwriter and director of her music videos, signed with Atlantic Records and I'll be able to go to Coachella and see her perform this year! She is called "The Lesbian Jesus" because she gathers people at her concerts and makes them feel safe and accepted. Son Thatcher has yet to find his footing, and I am so glad to be here and witness his self-discovery. I have a lot to live for and a new pump to nurture. When I sense the scope of my life, as I have on these pages, I know that Sarah will always be my true heart. I knew that first night. Sarah moved in with me when her 12-week ice show run was over. A couch, a mattress, boxes and various and sundry chairs arrived as part and parcel of the wonderful gift of Sarah's love. She left me alone the next day to go on tour with the show in Atlantic City. I guess it was up to me to decorate. So, I set about Feng-Shueing the joint and did some gigs with Mack. When Sarah returned, I had nothing on until the weekend. We set out on one of our many "Mini Vacances" to somewhere romantic and fun. Our life became one long date and when she bought the Alfa, in 1984, we took many top down trips up the coast, building on a romance beyond compare. After 5 years together, it was time to upgrade. I went to the jewelry district in downtown L.A. finally finding a diamond dealer that I trusted and after securing the goods. I went to a Cambodian jeweler for a custom ring and setting. Then I went to a lonely road in Marina Del Rey (yes, they exist). I paced off 20 feet south of a lifeguard tower and buried a champagne bottle packed in an ice wrap, two feet deep in the cold wet sand. I drove home.

Sarah returned from skating and had a late dinner. Around 11p.m. I suggested a walk
on the beach around. She squirmed a bit then concurred that a walk on the beach
would be a good way to herald in her birthday. It was much colder than we anticipated
so we grabbed jackets from the car. I've always thought that the slogan on California

license plates should be 'California – Bring a Sweater'. Anyway, we roamed onto the
Ice chilled sand until we were about 20 feet south of the lifeguard chair. That's when I spread our blanket on the sand and Sarah declined with the old, "It's too cold!" plea.

I insisted, promising that I would keep her warm. She may have thought that I wanted
to do that sex thing that we had grown to love so much but I wasn't in the mood anyway. I was in the mood to propose. So, I showed her the ring and asked if she would let me love her for the rest of our lives and she asked,
   "Can I keep my last name?"
I exhaled.
   "Of course."
Sarah delights me every day!
The question I'm most often asked when I see friends or when people that find out I've had a transplant is "My God, how are you feeling? Are you okay?" Well, to use a Dutch expression, of course. I'm okay. I'm so much better than okay. For the last decade I haven't been able to climb stairs without taking numerous breathless breaks.
While walking our dog Henry, I struggled to keep up with my quick-step walking wife.
My ejection fraction was 20% and slowly taking a medal winning nose-dive to 7%.
But now, I have a heart with an E.F. of 65%, a flight or two or three stairs doesn't faze
me and my wife often does manage to keep up with Henry and me. So, my heart is 46 and I'm going to be 70. The joke is: I'm 46 going on 70. I don't know whether to
Have a mid-life crisis or get a reverse mortgage. I wake up smiling at the new day I've
been given and I give a nod to my man, Bryan. Everything is magically festooned with
a fresh gossamer of expectation. When I drive, I drive with the windows open. I try to
make sure everyone I come in contact with feels a little better about being here with me, wherever we may be. Leaving a few laughs in my wake, as I course through the day, can't hurt and more importantly it entertains me. To say, I appreciate everything
a little more, is an under-statement. My wish came true. I'm the luckiest guy in the world and I'm loving my change of heart. Everything in life is more vivid, and it has an
edge. I strive each glorious day to meet life head on with the heart of a lion. After all, I'm living for two now…BE A HERO – DONATE

Mom and me in front of Grandpa Alcroft's 54 Packard

Grandpa Morgan, age 10, in his Hudson Twin -H-Power Buggy. Circa 1910

Linda, Cindy and Moi at the scene of Black Thursdays - 1958

143

Bedford school Days. Find me in the photo

!

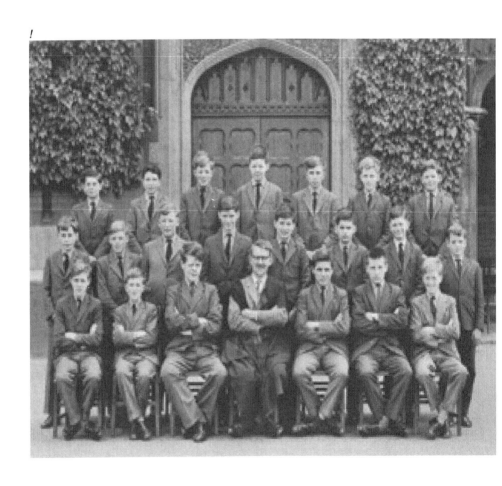

144

Colorado days at the former house

*The Silversmith who makes pretty
things with Tai Moon Mullins in Key West*

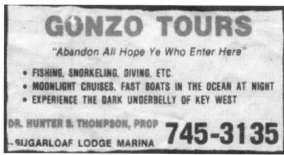

Gonzo Tours in 1978 Key West Yellow pages

My first time doing stand-up in Key West 1978

To much make-up for our first casino gig where I met Sarah, 1980

At the ICE HOUSE, our home club in L.A.

The first COMIC RELIEF…find us here, then find Phil Proctor

The Alfa…nuf said.

My wonderful children!

My wonderful Sarah!

The Special Olympic World Games with Greg.

My two scintillating views for 85 days

Our wonderful Henry, servicing me

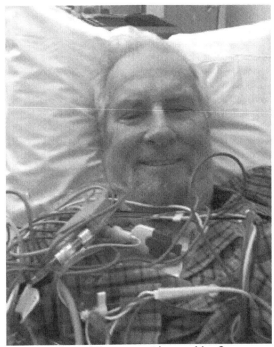

One of these must be working?

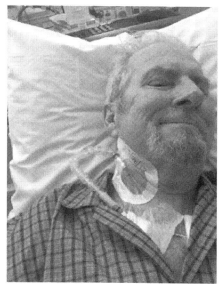

My Schvannz - Ganzz

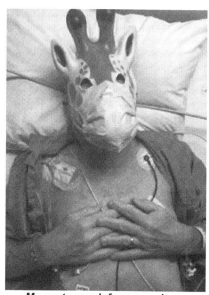

My go-to mask for procedures

Dr. Todo makes a liver pillow for me!

An experimental procedure?

A Fashion No-No

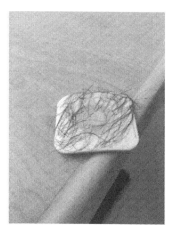

A Cedars Brazilian

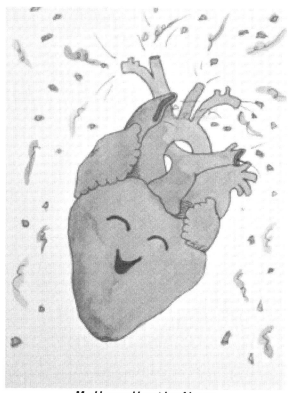

My Happy Heart by Alysse

My personal Tin Man dall.

ACKNOWLEDGEMENTS

Thanks to all of my angels of pure energy and love,, who kept me going.
They are listed below (in kinda' alphabetical order):

Sarah Kawahara and the Alcroft Kids, Alysse, Hayley, and Thatcher. Linda Alcroft (From New Jersey), Cindy Alcroft (From Ohio), Lance Aston and Marci Levy, Bob Bastanchury, Willy and Cathy Bietak, Steve Bluestein, Kris Caraway-Bowman, Chris Brochu, Lisa Carey and Judd Miller, Fritz Coleman, Bob and Lauren Dubac, Murphy Dunne, A.J. Eaton, Dave, Debbie and Jenny Eaton, Bob Fisher (my very first visitor), Eric Gersh, Dana Goldfarb and Barb Muskin, Linda and David Gonino (from Dallas), Jeannie Harrison, Kyle, and Sue Hefner, Scott Henderson, Shelley Herman, Dudley Herndon, Sam Herndon, Will Herndon, Valerie Johns, Bill Kates, Sue Kolinsky, Lisa Medway, Kristin Moser, Jack Mullins, Randy Lubas, Joanna Ng, Louise Palanker, Phil Proctor and Melinda Petersen, Tony and Luanne Quin, Bob Robinson, Jeff Sites, Robert and Laurie Slavin, Will Snyder, Mason Sommers, Gail Trace (from Cayucas), Eddie Yang, Ron Zonen.

ON THE PHONE - Bruce Wentworth (72 days in a row), Taffy Danoff, Terry and Gisela Head, Wendy Liebman, Ron Maranian, B.J. Martin, Jeannie McBride-Walla, Jeff Witjas.

My TINMAN DOLL dolls, Bob Rang and Michael Villegas.

ON MY WAVELENGTH - Sally Reno

BTW – Sarah got my family and me through this whole bad dream/good dream. She is a goddess and the strongest Ox that I know. My Soulmate, my savior.

COVER PHOTO – Sherry Coben

MY HEART TEAM:
Dr. Jon Kobashigawa
Dr. Jaime D. Moriguchi
Dr. Joshua Chung

155

Dr. Jignesh Patel
Dr. Michelle Kittleson
Dr. David Chang
Dr. Evan Kransdorf
Brenda Kearney
Nicole Ransbottom
Tina Kao
Onelegancy.org

MY LIVER TEAM:
When I asked my liver transplant surgeon Dr. Tsuyoshi Todo, for a list of those who helped, he responded: *Jamie, Congratulations on your talk (a TEDx talk I did at LACC) and thank you for being an advocate spreading the word about transplant and organ donation. Hopefully with this continued grassroots effort of targeting within the community, you will inspire more and more people to become donors.*

As you know, there was literally an army of people involved in your care at different steps of your progress that helped make your transplant a success.

Before the transplant, transplant nurses and coordinators who not only kept your listing status up to date with frequent labs checks, but also took calls in the middle of the night to arrange the timing, and transport for the donor team for your recovery operation. And our finance team that went and got clearance from your insurance to proceed with the transplant.

During the donor operation, from our center, the heart and liver recovery teams that went to get your organ. And the team of operating room staff that helped out with the recovery operation. In addition, a number of doctors, nurses, and healthcare professionals at the donor hospital that initially did their best to try to save your donor's life. Who in turn provided comfort to the donor's family when the donor became brain dead.

At our center, a number of operating room nurses, surgical technicians, perfusionists that ran the bypass machine, the blood bank staff that provided the needed blood and products you received during your operation, and the volunteers that donated their blood so we could use it during your operation.

There were also teams of Anesthesiologists for both the heart and liver portion that kept you alive while the surgeons worked to transplant your organs.

And after the operation, the army of ICU and hospital floor personnel, from nurses to pharmacists to clinical partners that helped you, to the sanitation staff that kept your room clean and food service that brought you your meals and the guys that came to draw your blood every morning.

There are probably no less than 100 people involved in your care from beginning to end. Not to mention your Transplant Cardiologists and Hepatologists that helped you get listed for a transplant in the first place.

Transplant is the ultimate team sport and I would be remiss to mention specific individuals. But rather I want to emphasize the tremendous teamwork involved getting safely out of the hospital and back into the wild.

We all are very happy with your successful transplant and take pride in the fact that we were able to be a part of your transplant. Thank you again for your continued work in raising awareness to the community for organ donation. And I hope we can continue this relationship so we keep engaging public together and promote more organ donations.

www.donatelife.net

34437369R00088

Made in the USA
Middletown, DE
25 January 2019